£1.00

The Busy World is Hushed

The Busy World is Hushed

Selected talks from BBC Radio 4

H Colin Davis

British Broadcasting Corporation

For Hope

Published by the
British Broadcasting Corporation
35 Marylebone High Street
London W1M 4AA

ISBN 0 563 177799

First published 1979

Printed in England
by Whitstable Litho,
Whitstable, Kent

Contents

Preface

At the end of 1973 during my term as Head of Religous Programmes, Radio, I invited H Colin Davis out to lunch and, over the pasta, suggested he should devise a series of Sunday-evening Epilogues from Palm Sunday to Advent, in which a theme would be illustrated with appropriate poetry, prose and music. He was clearly taken aback. He doubted his ability to undertake such a task and asked for a week to think about it. Six years, and over a hundred Epilogues later, a host of Radio 4 listeners are grateful for the pleasure he has given them Sunday by Sunday.

Working closely with Hubert Hoskins as producer, Barry Rose as music advisor and the BBC Singers, Colin has drawn upon his wide knowledge of literature, his love of the English language and his Christian faith to present certain truths about man and God. If some poets – Wordsworth, Hopkins, C Day Lewis, together with the King James's Bible – predominate, that is but a natural desire to share widely what gives him most joy, those insights he believes we too may find valuable and enduring.

Great St Mary's Church,
Cambridge

MICHAEL MAYNE

Introduction

Most of the people who are kind enough to write to me about my Sunday-night Epilogues on Radio 4, refer to the closing prayer with which they all end, saying how comforting it is and asking who wrote it. It was originally part of a sermon by Cardinal Newman and it seems to me to say everything that need be said at the end of the week when the busy world is hushed and before the fever of life starts up again on Monday morning. So instead of putting it at the end of each of the Epilogues reprinted here, I have put it at the end of the introduction.

People tend to address their letters to 'The Rev' and on one occasion the house rang with laughter when an envelope arrived for Canon Davis. I can, alas, claim no clerical or theological status. However, one of my favourite bedside books is the *Diary of the Reverend Francis Kilvert* and in it he asks himself the question 'Why do I keep this voluminous journal?' I find myself wholly in sympathy with his answer:

> Partly because life appears to me such a curious and wonderful thing that it almost seems a pity that even such a humble and uneventful life as mine should pass altogether away without some such record as this, and partly too because I think the record may amuse and interest some who come after me.

In an infinitely smaller and humbler way I hope that these talks in their printed form may interest and give pleasure to a wider circle than the faithful few who have stayed up so late each Sunday night to listen to them.

I have drawn on a fairly wide range of poetry and prose, to llustrate my basic themes. My reflections and comments on hem have been thoroughly vetted by my wife who has an unering instinct for obscurity, pomposity and excessive self-esteem.

H COLIN DAVIS

O Lord, support us all the day long of this troublous life, until the shades lengthen, the evening comes, the busy world is hushed, the fever of life is over, and our work is done. Then, Lord, in they mercy, grant us safe lodging, a holy rest, and peace at the last, through Jesus Christ our Lord.

CARDINAL NEWMAN

When I was a child, I spake as a child, I understood as a child, I thought as a child, but when I became a man I never completely succeeded in putting off childish things. I still enjoy a childish game called The Parson's Cat which we used to play with the children – and still do with our grandchildren – to pass the time on long journeys. The Parson's Cat is an amiable cat, The Parson's Cat is a beastly cat, and so on in turn, pointlessly and interminably, until the exhausted animal became zealous, zestful or plain zany.

And so The Parson's Cat has given me an idea for a series of Epilogues – a hook on which to hang my thoughts. 'A' is for Alleluia. I am alpha, the beginning, the beginning of the new dispensation of the arisen Christ.

Around Easter time in the church calendar it is customary to celebrate another beginning – 'A' also stands for Annunciation. The first link in that chain of events outlined in the creed with the words 'conceived by the Holy Ghost' which led up to the climax of 'the third day He rose again.'

No subject captured the imagination of the Italian painters of the Renaissance more compellingly than the Annunciation – the confrontation between Mary the simple Jewish girl and the resplendent Gabriel – the angel of the Lord. How little she realised the tremendous significance of his message and how after all the dramas of the birth and ministry and death of her son she must have looked back to that peaceful spring morning where it all began.

There was never a morning quite so tremendous
again.
The birth, you think? I'm not for setting great
store
By birth. Births aren't beginnings. And anyway
She only wanted to sleep off the pain
Which had made her a beast among beasts on the
cow-house floor.

Shepherds and magnates tiptoeing through the hay
(You get all kinds at an inn, she drowsily thought),
Even the babe – they were part of a snowdrift
trance,
Almost unreal. He was to prove a good son
In his way, though his way was beyond her.
Whatever he sought
When he left home and led his friends such a
dance,
He did not forget her as other boys might have
done.

Her morning of mornings was when one flew to
bring
Some news that changed her cottage into a queen's
Palace; the table she worked at shone like gold.
And in the orchard it is suddenly spring,
All bird and blossom and fresh-painted green.
What was it the grand visitor foretold
Which made earth heaven for a village Mary?
He was saying something about a Saviour Prince,
But she only heard him say, 'You will bear a child',
And that was why the spring came. Angels carry
Such tidings often enough, but never since
To one who in such blissful ignorance smiled.

C DAY LEWIS *Annunciation:Leonardo*

'And in the orchard it is suddenly spring.' However early or late Easter falls its celebration marks the end of winter – a spiritual as well as a physical sense of rebirth – especially if the weather is kind and you wake up to one of those magical spring days like the one described in a poem by Ted Hughes.

Blue haze. Bees hanging in air at the hive-mouth.
Crawling in prone stupor of sun
On the hive-lip. Snowdrops. Two buzzards,
Still-wings, each
Magnetised to the other
Float orbits.
Cattle standing warm. Lit, happy stillness.
A raven, under the hill,
Coughing among bare oaks.
Aircraft, elated, splitting blue.
Leisure to stand. The knee-deep mud at the trough
Stiffening. Lambs freed to be foolish.

The earth invalid, dropsied, bruised, wheeled
Out into the sun,
After the frightful operation.
She lies back, wounds undressed to the sun,
To be healed,
Sheltered from the sneapy chill creeping North
   wind,
Leans back, eyes closed, exhausted, smiling
Into the sun. Perhaps dozing a little.
While we sit, and smile, and wait, and know
She is not going to die.

TED HUGHES *March Morning Unlike Others*

In an essay which he called 'The Best Picture' Aldous Huxley described a hair-raising seven-hour bus journey up and down the Apennines to the small and not very interesting town of Borgo

San Sepolcro with its one vile hotel simply to see one picture – Piero Della Francesca's marvellous fresco of the Resurrection. Filling the foreground are four sleeping soldiers leaning against the side of the sepulchre, out of which the majestic figure of the risen Christ is climbing with a tremendous sense of purpose and vigour, the still bleeding wound in His side the only reminder of all that had gone before. In the background are stylised trees and rocks and a dawn sky, and a sense of absolute stillness and calm – as moving as that felt by Wordsworth on Westminster bridge.

> Never did sun more beautifully steep
> In his first splendour, valley, rock or hill,
> Ne'er saw I, never felt, a calm so deep.

Aldous Huxley's judgment of it as the best picture in the world was an aesthetic one and, to him, his long and arduous journey before the days of instant travel was no hardship for such a rewarding artistic experience.

It could also be said to be the best picture in the world because it expresses as perhaps no other painter had done 'the might, majesty, dominion and power' of the risen Christ. To discover that power is for some people also a long and arduous journey and for others an instant experience, but at whatever stage of the journey we find ourselves we celebrate the Resurrection of the Son of God. 'A' is for Alleluia.

B

Truly the light is sweet and a pleasant thing it is to behold the sun.
But if a man live many years and rejoice in them all;
Yet let him remember the days of darkness; for they shall be many.

ECCLESIASTES 11.7

The letter 'B' instantly conjures up for me the word 'battle'. It is one that suggests a conflict of ideas – beauty and the beast, birth and bereavement, blindness and beholding.

The word 'behold' would be considered archaic these days. It occurs frequently in the Authorised Version of the Bible but has, of course, largely disappeared from our modern translations, thereby diminishing them, because it is a splendid and powerful word. 'Behold, the hand-maid of the Lord', 'Behold, I stand at the gate', 'Behold, the man' . . . It is a word which shakes us out of our spiritual blindness and makes us look outwards and upwards.

Lift up your eyes on high, and behold who hath created these things . . .
Hast thou not known? Hast thou not heard, that the everlasting God, the Lord, the creator of the ends of the earth, fainteth not, neither is weary?
There is no searching of his understanding.
He giveth power to the faint; and to them that have no might he increaseth strength.
Even the youths shall faint and be weary, and the young men shall utterly fall.

But they that wait upon the Lord shall renew their strength; they shall mount up with wings as eagles, they shall run and not be weary, and they shall walk and not faint.

ISAIAH 40. 26, 28-30

We all suffer from spiritual blindness but it is impossible to imagine what it must be like to be born physically blind. Never to see the sky and clouds, never to see trees or flowers however heightened the other senses may be in compensation. Only to hear a loving voice, never to see a loving face. How on earth can you describe to the blind a rainbow, or a painting by Turner, or the baptistry window in Coventry Cathedral? If you read poetry to them what images do they form?

The rainbow comes and goes,
And lovely is the rose;
The moon doth with delight
Look round her when the heavens are bare;
  Waters on a starry night
  Are beautiful and fair;
The sunshine is a glorious birth;
But yet I know, wher'er I go,
That there hath passed away a glory from the earth.

WILLIAM WORDSWORTH from
Ode on Intimations of Immortality

There is a lovely picture by Millais called 'The Blind Girl'. In the background there is a double rainbow against the black clouds of a receding storm, but the sun has broken through to suffuse the wet grass of a hayfield in the middle distance with an intense lemon-green light. In the centre of the foreground a blind beggar-girl sits by the side of the road, her head thrown back, drinking in the warmth of the sunshine through her closed eyes. She has a look of serene contentment and peace as though that ancient plea to the Holy Spirit was being answered:

Enable with perpetual light
The dulness of our blinded sight:
Anoint and cheer our soiled face
With the abundance of thy grace.

There is one more element in the composition of the picture which I have not mentioned. Sitting with the sun-worshipping blind girl, clasping her hand, is a younger girl companion even more shabbily dressed than she is. She can *see* all this radiant colour and beauty and yet is quite unmoved by it; she is clearly bored and restless and wanting to get on.

Like her, we take our sight and hearing for granted and because they are there most of us only half use them. We constantly 'miss the many-splendoured thing' like that flat-footed fellow in one of Wordsworth's less felicitous poems:

A primrose by a river's brim
A yellow primrose was to him,
And it was nothing more.

And yet the poet Edward Thomas with his sensitive and observant eye could find beauty and significance in a weed-choked corner of an abandoned farm-yard.

Tall nettles cover up, as they have done
These many springs, the rusty harrow, the plough
Long worn out, and the roller made of stone:
Only the elm tree butt tops the nettles now.

This corner of the farmyard I like most:
As well as any bloom upon a flower
I like the dust on the nettles, never lost
Except to prove the sweetness of a shower.

EDWARD THOMAS *Tall Nettles*

The theme of blindness both spiritual and physical is a recurring one in the book of Isaiah and it is echoed in the Gospels. When Christ returned to Galilee 'in the power of the spirit' He went to His home in Nazareth and it was in the synagogue there that He chose to read such a passage from the book of Isaiah.

> The Spirit of the Lord is upon me because he hath anointed me to preach the gospel to the poor; he hath sent me to heal the broken hearted, to preach deliverance to the captives and recovering of sight to the blind, to set at liberty them that are bruised.
>
> LUKE 4.18

Of all the accounts of Christ's healing powers the most moving is that of the blind man at Bethsaida and this is because he is not instantly cured. At first he sees shadowy figures and it is only when Christ puts His sensitive hands on his eyes a second time that everything comes into focus.

> And he cometh to Bethsaida; and they bring a blind man unto him, and besought him to touch him.
> And he took the blind man by the hand, and led him out of the town; and when he had spit on his eyes, and put his hands upon him, he asked him if he saw ought.
> And he looked up, and said, I see men as trees walking.
> After that he put his hands again upon his eyes, and made him look up; and he was restored, and saw every man clearly.
>
> MARK 8.22-25

The letter 'C' suggests to me a whole succession of lovely-sounding words – many of them with a rather old-fashioned ring, though none the worse for that. Strong words like 'courage' and 'chivalry' and 'concern'. Gentle ones like 'courtesy' and 'contentment' and 'contemplation'. Out of such a box of delights I am going to pick three and the first of them is that rare but splendid quality – 'compassion'.

Unlike the Good Samaritan who had compassion on his fellow traveller who had been beaten up, it is so much easier not to get involved, not to call in the police, and so, like the priest and the Levite we pass by on the other side as we make the journey along our own particular road to Jericho. We are what the psychologists now call 'unresponsive bystanders'.

> But a certain Samaritan, as he journeyed, came where he was: and when he saw him he had compassion on him, and went to him, and bound up his wounds, pouring in oil and wine, and set him on his own beast, and brought him to an inn, and took care of him.
> And on the morrow when he departed, he took out two pence and gave them to the host, and said unto him, Take care of him; whatsoever thou spendest more, when I come again, I will repay thee.
>
> LUKE 10.33-35

Another equally compassionate man was St Martin of Tours; a

soldier's son and himself an officer in the Roman army of occupation in Gaul in the fourth century.

One cold January morning, when stationed at Amiens, he saw a naked beggar shivering at the side of the road and had compassion on him and cutting his warm military cloak in two with his sword gave half of it to him. Soon after he was baptised and asked for release from military service saying, 'I am Christ's soldier. I am not allowed to fight'. Such an act of courage was inevitably seen as cowardice, but he was grudgingly given his discharge when he countered by offering to stand unarmed between the opposing lines.

Martin went on to become a bishop and one of the great missionaries of the early church. It is said that he once had a dream in which our Lord appeared to him in the half of his soldier's cloak which he had given to the beggar and like St Francis he is one of the patron saints of the halt and the lame. And that is why above the great west door of the chapel of Chailey Heritage in Sussex, where for over seventy years handicapped children have been shown compassion, there is a stone carving of St Martin curbing his horse as he raises his sword to slash his cloak in two for the poor creature kneeling at his feet.

Related to compassion is my second word, another rather old-fashioned one which could be revived with profit and which is one of the key words in the marriage ceremony. The verb to cherish – 'to love and to cherish till death us do part' – which is so all-embracing in its meaning of keeping a marriage alive and in good repair when the first fine careless rapture is over. Nowadays it is so easy to dissolve the union before it has had a chance to mature, to be tested both in prosperity and adversity, and so to become over the years a relationship less exciting perhaps, but infinitely more sustaining.

> This is not Love perhaps – Love that lays down
> Its life, that many waters cannot quench, nor
>   the floods drown –

But something written in lighter ink, said in a
lower tone:
Something perhaps especially our own:
A need at times to be together and talk –
And then the finding we can walk
More firmly through dark narrow places
And meet more easily nightmare faces:
A need to reach out sometimes hand to hand,
And then find Earth less like an alien land:
A need for alliance to defeat
The whisperers at the corner of the street:
A need for inns on roads, islands in seas, halts for
discoveries to be shared,
Maps checked and notes compared:
A need at times of each for each
Direct as the need of throat and tongue for speech.

A J S TESSIMOND *Not Love Perhaps*

The words 'compassion' and 'cherish' both have, as it were, a positive charge, but my third has a negative one – the archaic but powerful verb, to be cumbered. A word which has great relevance in the fever of life today.

In the New English Bible account of the occasion when Jesus arrived (I suspect unannounced) for a meal in the house of Martha and Mary, it says that Martha was 'distracted by her many tasks'. The Authorised Version puts it so much more graphically when it says that she was 'cumbered about much serving'. And the word is also used in that torrent of alliteration which Gerard Manley Hopkins pours out in his poem 'The Leaden Echo and the Golden Echo' in which he is seeking to find some purpose in the rat-race:

O then, weary then why should we tread?
O why are we so haggard at the heart, so
care-coiled, care-killed, so fagged, so fashed, so
cogged, so cumbered . . .

And while poor Martha was so cumbered about much serving Mary was finding the answer as she sat at the feet of her master who must surely have said to her:

> Take no thought, saying, What shall we eat? or, What shall we drink? or, Wherewithal shall we be clothed? (For after all these things do the Gentiles seek:) for your heavenly Father knoweth that ye have need of all these things. But seek ye first the kingdom of God, and his righteousness; and all these things shall be added unto you. Take therefore no thought for the morrow: for the morrow shall take thought for the things of itself. Sufficient unto the day is the evil thereof.
>
> MATTHEW 6.31-34

Most of us are cumbered in our minds about much serving, about the mechanics of living: but we are also cumbered in our hearts by fears and doubts which pronouncements by clever theologians may increase rather than dispel.

I find myself refreshingly *un*cumbered when I listen to the comfortable words of an old French mystic who wrote three hundred years ago:

> True devotion does not consist in reasoning and speculation and a lot of brain-work, but in submission and humility of the heart which, being joined with love, not only unites the heart with God, but brings as well a great enlightening, for divine love is a clear fire from which men receive great abundance of exalted thoughts: so much so that it is a bad mistake to cumber the mind with one's efforts to teach it too much. Love is an ever flowing river which carries treasures of understanding and knowledge gently to the soul.
>
> JOHN JOSEPH SURIN
> *An Anthology of Mysticism*

The letter 'D' has for me ominous overtones in the minor key – dreadful words instantly begin to queue up in my mind – devils and demons, death and decay, doubt and defeat, and the darkness and despondency of the Psalmist with his despairing cry:

> How long wilt thou forget me, O Lord, for ever: how long wilt thou hide thy face from me?
> How long shall I seek counsel in my soul, and be so vexed in my heart: how long shall mine enemies triumph over me?
>
> PSALM 13.1-2

I think the letter 'D' is one that must have had a special appeal for John Bunyan; because it is in *Pilgrim's Progress* that he describes how Christian travelled from the City of Destruction, through the Slough of Despond to Doubting Castle, the owner whereof was Giant Despair, who had a wife whose name was Diffidence, and who put him in a dark Dungeon. Then the key changes into the major. For just as Christian, trusting in God's mercy, at last escapes from Doubting Castle and comes to the Delectable Mountains where he catches his first glimpse of the Celestial City, so the Psalmist at last shakes off his despondency and, regaining his faith, cries out:

> But I have trusted in thy mercy; my heart shall rejoice in Thy salvation.
>
> PSALM 13.5

In one of his longer narrative poems, Browning describes how in the sixteenth century, Paracelsus, a doctor-cum-scientist-cum-charlatan (of whom there are plenty of counterparts today) spent his whole time travelling round the world in search of knowledge. And as he finally lies dying, he realises bitterly that his life has been wasted : because in his arrogant assumption of his own superior wisdom he has failed to love his fellow-men, failed to appreciate that they too are all searching for the Way, the Truth and the Life, however faltering their steps.

In my own heart love had not been made wise
To trace love's faint beginnings in mankind,
To know even hate is but a mask of love's,
To see a good in evil, and a hope
In ill-success; to sympathise, be proud
Of their half-reasons, faint aspirings, dim
Struggles for truth, their poorest fallacies,
Their prejudice and fears and cares and doubts;
All with a touch of nobleness, despite
Their error, upward tending all though weak,
Like plants in mines which never saw the sun,
But dream of him, and guess where he may be,
And do their best to climb and get to him.
All this I knew not, and I failed . . .

And yet his final words are not of failure and defeat but a great affirmation of faith and hope for the future which we, in our moments of despondency, can share with him.

. . . If I stoop
Into a dark tremendous sea of cloud,
It is but for a time; I press God's lamp
Close to my breast; its splendour, soon or late,
Will pierce the gloom: I shall emerge one day.

ROBERT BROWNING from *Paracelsus*

So, not all words beginning with 'D' are dismal ones. From the dark Dungeon of Giant Despair Christian reached the Delectable Mountains; and when we fight off despondency and emerge from the dark, tremendous sea of cloud, we can once again give ourselves up to delight and thank God for the catalogue of delights which the world can still unfold. And surely there can be no more satisfying a one than the list of things which Charles Lamb hoped, rather wistfully, would not die with him:

> Sun, and sky, and solitary walks, and summer holidays, and the greenness of fields, and the delicious juices of meats and fishes, and society, and the cheerful glass, and candlelight, and fireside conversations and innocent vanities, and jests, and irony itself – do these things go out with life?
>
> CHARLES LAMB *Essays of Elia*

My last two words in this galaxy of 'Ds' are devotion and duty, which apply especially to St George, the Patron Saint of England and of all soldiers. It seems unlikely that he ever rescued a maiden from a dragon. But he *is* a symbol of devotion and duty, a symbol that there are still dragons to slay – more dragons though perhaps fewer maidens than in his day.

One of Rudyard Kipling's last poems is called 'The Storm-Cone'. It was written in 1932, when armed men were beginning to spring up from the dragons' teeth which we had sown at Versailles, and which lead inevitably to the Second World War. We survived that storm; but the prophetic warning which he gave of dangers ahead still holds good today.

> This is the midnight – let no star
> Delude us – dawn is very far.
> This is the tempest long foretold –
> Slow to make head but sure to hold.

Stand by! The lull 'twixt blast and blast
Signals the storm is near not past;
And worse than present jeopardy
May our forlorn tomorrow be.

If we have cleared the expectant reef,
Let no man look for his relief.
Only the darkness hides the shape
Of further peril to escape.

It is decreed that we abide
The weight of gale against the tide
And those huge waves the outer main
Sends in to set us back again.

They fall and whelm. We strain to hear
The pulses of her labouring gear,
Till the deep throb beneath her proves
After each shudder and check, she moves!

She moves, with all save purpose lost,
To make her offing from the coast;
But, till she fetches open sea,
Let no man deem that he is free!

RUDYARD KIPLING *The Storm-Cone*

The spirit of the Lord shall rest upon him, the spirit of wisdom and understanding; the spirit of counsel and might, the spirit of knowledge and of the fear of the Lord.

ISIAH 11.2

Come hither, and I shall light a candle of understanding in thine heart which shall not be put out.

2 ESDRAS 14.25

Having now come to the letter 'E' let us resist the desire to luxuriate in emotion or excellence or ecstasy; or to wallow in evil or envy or execration; because I have chosen, surprisingly perhaps, the fashionable word 'empathy', which doesn't even appear in my ageing Oxford dictionary.

The Penguin dictionary on the other hand defines it rather well as 'the ability fully to understand and share another's feeling', which gives it a deeper, more all-embracing sense than the old-fashioned word 'sympathy' with its slightly mawkish overtones and suggestion of floral tributes.

Empathy is a timeless quality and knows no bounds of age or social standing or sex. It is, though, an essential ingredient of an enduring marriage like Robert Browning's to Elizabeth Barrett, which Elizabeth expressed so movingly in one of her 'Sonnets from the Portuguese'.

How do I love thee? Let me count the ways.

I love thee to the depth and breadth and height
My soul can reach, when feeling out of sight
For the ends of Being and Ideal grace.
I love thee to the level of everyday's
Most quiet need, by sun and candlelight.
I love thee freely, as men strive for right;
I love thee purely as they turn from praise.
I love thee with the passion put to use
In my old griefs, and with my childhood's faith.
I love thee with a love I seemed to lose
With my lost saints, – I love thee with the breath,
Smiles, tears, of all my life! – And, if God choose,
I shall but love thee better after death.

ELIZABETH BROWNING *Sonnets from the Portuguese*

Empathy is a quality which children instantly recognise in certain older people – even improbable people like poor, sad, lonely, epileptic Edward Lear who wrote such enchanting poetry for them; a quality which Queen Victoria found in Disraeli but not in Gladstone. It was the bond between David and Jonathan; and the Authorised Version records that 'the soul of Jonathan was knit with the soul of David, and Jonathan loved him as his own soul'. It was the tie which made it impossible for Ruth to leave her mother-in-law, Naomi, when she returned as a widow from Moab to her own country:

And Ruth said, Intreat me not to leave thee, or to return from following after thee: for whither thou goest, I will go; and where thou lodgest, I will lodge: thy people shall be my people, and thy God my God:
Where thou diest, will I die, and there will I be buried: the Lord do so to me, and more also, if ought but death part thee and me.

RUTH 1.16-17

Solomon's attitude towards Israel is an example of empathy in its widest Churchillian sense of sharing and understanding the feelings of a whole people – the young nation entrusted to his care by his father, David.

The Lord appears to Solomon in a dream and asks him what gifts He shall give him, and his reply pleases the Lord:

> I am but a little child: I know not how to go out or come in. Give therefore thy servant an understanding heart to judge Thy people, that I may discern between good and bad; for who is able to judge this thy so great a people?
>
> I KINGS 3.7-9

The supreme example of empathy is that of Christ in His encounters with the ordinary men and women and children whom He met on his journeys up and down Palestine – the woman of Samaria when she comes to draw water at Jacob's well; Mary, the sister of poor kitchen-bound Martha, who sat at Jesus' feet and heard His word; and the two bewildered and dispirited disciples who walk to Emmaus after the death of their master and are joined by this stranger who seemed so 'fully to understand and share' their feelings.

> And it came to pass, as he sat at meat with them, he took bread, and blessed it, and brake, and gave to them.
> And their eyes were opened, and they knew him; and he vanished out of their sight.
> And they said one to another, Did not our heart burn within us, while he talked with us by the way, and while he opened to us the scriptures?
>
> LUKE 24.30-32

The English Larousse gives the word 'empathy' a further dimension when it describes it as 'the power to enter into emotional harmony with a work of art.

Perhaps the most hauntingly beautiful expression of this sort of empathy is that of the poet Keats when contemplating the timeless beauty of the pagan festival portrayed on a Grecian urn.

Thou still unravished bride of quietness,
Thou foster-child of silence and slow time,
Sylvan historian, who canst thus express
A flowery tale more sweetly than our rhyme:
What leaf-fringed legend haunts about thy shape
Of deities or mortals, or of both,
In Tempe or the vales of Arcady?
What men or gods are these? What maidens loth?
What mad pursuit? What struggle to escape?
What pipes and timbrels? What mad ecstasy?

Heard melodies are sweet, but those unheard
Are sweeter; therefore, ye soft pipes, play on;
Not to the sensual ear, but, more endeared,
Pipe to the spirit ditties of no tone:
Fair youth, beneath the trees, thou canst not leave
Thy song, nor ever can those trees be bare;
Bold lover, never, never canst thou kiss,
Though winning near the goal – yet do not grieve;
She cannot fade, though thou hast not thy bliss,
For ever wilt thou love and she be fair!

And the poem ends with his great affirmation of the sustaining power of all works of art – poetry, painting, sculpture, music – which is handed on from one generation to another.

When old age shall this generation waste,
Thou shalt remain, in midst of other woe
Than ours, a friend to man, to whom thou sayst,
'Beauty is truth, truth beauty, – that is all
Ye know on earth, and all ye need to know.'

KEATS from *Ode to a Grecian Urn*

In the fear of the Lord is strong confidence:
And his children shall have a place of refuge.
The fear of the Lord is a fountain of life;
To depart from the snares of death.

PROVERBS 14.26-27

The Lord is my light and my salvation; whom shall I fear?
The Lord is the strength of my life; of whom shall I be afraid?

PSALM 27.1

Yea, though I walk through the valley of the shadow of death,
I will fear no evil: For thou art with me . . .

PSALM 23.4

The word 'fear' has two quite distinct meanings. Firstly what my dictionary defines as 'a feeling of reverence and awe'. 'The fear of the Lord is the beginning of wisdom'.

And secondly, as 'the emotion of pain or uneasiness caused by the sense of impending danger'.

The words 'fear', 'fearsome' and 'afraid' occur frequently throughout the Old and New Testaments, from the moment when, in his guilt, Adam was afraid when he heard the voice of God, walking in the garden in the cool of the day. The shepherds, keeping watch over their flocks, were afraid when the glory of the Lord shone about them, proclaiming the Birth of Christ. The disciples were often afraid. They 'cried out for fear', when the storm blew up on the lake of Galilee, and Christ, walking on the water, said: 'Be of good cheer, it is I. Be not afraid'. And when He exorts them to take heed for the morrow, to seek no earthly riches, but the kingdom of God, He says: 'Fear not, little flock; for it is your Father's good pleasure to give you the kingdom'.

But when Christ was arrested, and taken away to be tried and crucified on that first Good Friday Christ's little flock were mortally afraid and fled into hiding.

> Good Friday in my heart! Fear and affright!
> My thoughts are the disciples when they fled
> My words – the words that priest and soldier said
> My deed – the spear to desecrate the dead.
> And day, thy death therein, is changed to night.

Even when Jesus Himself stood in the midst of them after His Resurrection, with the reassuring greeting, 'Peace be with you', Luke describes how the disciples were 'terrified and afraid' until at last the tremendous truth dawned on them.

> Then Easter in my heart sends up the sun.
> My thoughts are Mary, when she turned to see,
> My words are Peter, answering, 'Lovest thou me?'
> My deeds are all thine own drawn close to thee,
> And night and day, since thou dost rise, are one.

MARY COLERIDGE *Good Friday*

Just as the disciples were terrified and afraid of arrest – at the hands of the authorities – for their beliefs, so all down the centuries people have had to live in fear like the brave Czechs and Poles today, and the countless prisoners of conscience in so many other countries in which evil regimes have tried to destroy the spirit of freedom, countries in which no neighbour can be trusted, and the knock on the door is a sound to be feared.

Last night they came across the river and
Entered the city. Women were awake
With lights and food. They entertained the band,
Not asking what the men had come to take
Or what strange tongue they spoke
Or why they came so suddenly through the land.

Now in the morning all the town is filled
With stories of the swift and dark invasion;
The women say that not one stranger told
A reason for his coming. The intrusion
Was not for devastation:
Peace is apparent still on hearth and field.

Yet all the city is a haunted place.
Man meeting man speaks cautiously. Old friends
Close up the candid looks upon their face.
There is no warmth in hands accepting hands;
Each ponders, 'Better hide myself in case
Those strangers have set up their homes in minds
I used to walk in. Better draw the blinds
Even if the strangers haunt in my own house.'

ELIZABETH JENNINGS *The Enemies*

This country has been spared the ordeal of enemy occupation for over nine hundred years; and we still have freedom of speech, but surely not one of us can claim freedom from every form of fear. It is part of the human condition, and not a cause for guilt. There is the physiological fear that warns of impending danger. In his book, *Pyrenean*, J B Morton describes how, as a young man, he walked all alone that formidable mountain barrier from the Mediterranean to the Atlantic.

One day he set out to cross a particularly steep and desolate pass, and in the afternoon a storm blew up and the mists suddenly came down, and he realised that he had lost his sense of direction.

As men will when they are frightened, I went on faster than ever, determined to get myself out of this mess, and forgetting the danger, in such circumstances, of exhaustion. All this while the mist blanketed me and the rain soaked me; and after a time, I discovered that I was walking on shale and that there was no sign of a path. These adventures and perils are the rewards of travel and when one is safe out of them, it is pleasant to boast and to embroider the story; but the actual experience, the living of the thing gives one the chill of death. Strength and youth are of no avail, for a man may go on walking round and round in the mist until he drops; or he may walk over a precipice; or he may go mad . . . As I stared this way and that into the impenetrable mist, the full sense of the hazard of the business in hand overwhelmed me for a moment, and I prayed silently that I might not lose my head, and become panic-stricken. Then, gripping my staff, I set off across the rough ground, stepping carefully, and watching for a rift in the clouds.

J B MORTON *Pyrenean*

But it is the irrational fears of the mind and imagination which are even more sapping – the nightmare terrors in which there is no rift in the clouds. Terrors which Gerard Manley Hopkins experienced and described with such haunting imagery when he wrote:

O the mind, mind has mountains; cliffs of fall
Frightful, sheer, no-man-fathomed . . .

Fear of death, fear of life, fear of the unknown – they are all recurring themes in the Book of Psalms; and perhaps nowhere are they dispelled with such comfort and reassurance as in the words of the ninety-first Psalm.

He that dwelleth in the secret place of the most High shall abide under the shadow of the Almighty.

I will say of the Lord, He is my refuge and my fortress: my God; in him will I trust.
Surely he shall deliver thee from the snare of the fowler and from the noisome pestilence.
He shall cover thee with his feathers, and under his wings shalt thou trust; his truth shall be thy shield and buckler.
There shall no evil befall thee, neither shall any plague come nigh thy dwelling.
For he shall give his angels charge over three, to keep thee in all thy ways.

God Almighty first planted a garden and indeed it is the purest of human pleasures. It is the greatest refreshment to the spirits of man; without which buildings and palaces are but gross handiworks.

FRANCIS BACON *Essay on Gardens*

. . .

And God said, let the earth bring forth grass, and the earth brought forth grass, and herb yielding seed after his kind, and the trees yielding fruit whose seed was in itself after his kind, and God saw that it was good.

GENESIS 1.11-12

. . .

And the Lord God planted a garden eastward in Eden; and there He put the man whom he had formed. And out of the ground made the Lord to grow every tree that is pleasant to the sight and good for food; the tree of life also in the midst of the garden and the tree of knowledge of good and evil.

GENESIS 2.8-9

. . .

Jesus went forth with his disciples over the brook Kedron where was a garden into which he entered, and his disciples.

And he was withdrawn from them about a stone's cast, and kneeled down and prayed, saying: 'Father, if thou be willing, remove this cup from me; nevertheless not my will but thine be done.'
And there appeared unto him an angel from Heaven, strengthening him:

LUKE 22.14-43

. . .

Now in the place where he was crucified there was a garden; and in the garden a new sepulchre, wherein was never man yet laid. There laid they Jesus . . . for the sepulchre was nigh at hand.

JOHN 19.41-42

. . .

Mary stood without at the sepulchre weeping . . . Jesus saith unto her, Woman, why weepest thou? Whom seekest thou? She, supposing him to be the gardener, saith unto him, Sir, if thou have borne him hence, tell me where thou hast laid him, and I will take him away. Jesus saith unto her, Mary. She turned herself and saith unto him 'Rabboni', which is to say 'Master!'

JOHN 20.11-16

By now it will be clear that in my alphabet 'G' stands for gardens. Three gardens have a special significance in the unfolding narrative of the Bible. The first is the earthly paradise, the Garden of Eden in which man first sins so that it becomes the garden of disgrace. The second is the Garden of Gethsemane in which Christ overcomes the final temptation to escape His trial and death by which He might atone for that sin – the garden of resolution. And the third is the garden of Calvary, where Mary first sees the risen Lord – the garden of resurrection.

It seems strange that there is not a fourth garden of the heavenly paradise, but the imagery used to describe the new heaven and the new earth in the Book of Revelation is strictly urban – a walled city with pearly entrance gates, its streets paved with gold; a place with many mansions, a place where there shall be no more sea. It seems stranger that the English, with their obsessive love of gardens and the sea, should have accepted this inland and municipal bias – to say nothing of the appalling monotony of its weather pattern – which they have expressed so frequently in their hymns.

> There no cloud nor passing vapour
> Dims the brightness of the air.
> Endless noonday, glorious noonday
> From the sun of suns is there.
> There no night brings rest from labour
> For unknown are toil and care.

Not a very 'lovesome' prospect and a very far cry from the paradise envisaged in most Eastern writings.

The word 'paradise' comes from the Persian, and was used to describe the rural parks and pleasure gardens of the Persian kings. They imagined for themselves the after life as a cool, shady oasis in delightful contrast with the frightful heat of the 'endless noonday' of their daily life.

> How the earth burns! Each pebble underfoot
> Is as a living thing with power to wound.
> The white sand quivers, and the footfall mute
> Of the slow camels strikes but gives no sound,
> As though they walked on flame, not solid ground.
> 'Tis noon, and the beasts' shadows even have fled
> Back to their feet, and there is fire around
> And fire beneath, and overhead the sun.

Pitiful heaven! What is this we view?
Tall trees, a river, pools, where swallows fly,
Thickets of oleander where doves coo,
Shades deep as midnight, greenness for tired eyes.
Hark, how the light winds in the palm-tops sigh.
Oh this is rest. Oh this is paradise.

WILFRED SCAWEN BLUNT *The Oasis of Sidi Khaled*

The exact nature of this final garden of paradise, or whatever form of words is used to describe the after life, is a mystery which every man must explore for himself; but that it leads on ultimately from the garden of the resurrection is the basis of Christian hope.

Most children, but alas not all, experience for a time the green and carefree delights of the first garden with its innocent pleasures so aptly described by Thomas Traherne:

> I knew not that there were any sins, or complaints or laws. I dreamed not of poverties, contentions or vices. All tears and quarrels were hidden from my eyes.
> In the absence of these I was entertained like an Angel with the works of God in their splendour and glory; I saw all in the peace of Eden.

Most older people, and not just the saints and heroes, have to walk at some time in their own Garden of Gethsemane, hoping that the cup might pass. And like the pathetic young soldier of the first war in Kipling's poem, one prays that they may be conscious of an angel strengthening them.

The Garden called Gethsemane
  In Picardy it was,
And there the people came to see
  The English soldiers pass.
We used to pass – we used to pass
Or halt as it might be,

And ship our masks in case of gas
  Beyond Gethsemane.

The Garden called Gethsemane,
  It held a pretty lass
But all the time she talked to me
  I prayed my cup might pass.
The officer sat on the chair,
  The men lay on the grass,
And all the time we halted there
  I prayed my cup might pass.

It didn't pass – it didn't pass –
It didn't pass from me.
I drank it when we met the gas
Beyond Gethsemane!

RUDYARD KIPLING *Gethsemane*

Behold, I stand at the door, and knock: if any man hear my voice, and open the door, I will come in to him, and will sup with him, and he with me.

REVELATION 3.20

Now it came to pass, as they went, that he entered into a certain village: and a certain woman named Martha received him into her house. And she had a sister called Mary, which also sat at Jesus' feet, and heard his word.
But Martha was cumbered about much serving, and came to him, and said, Lord, dost thou not care that my sister hath left me to serve alone? bid her therefore that she help me.
And Jesus answered and said unto her, Martha, Martha, thou art careful and troubled about many things: But one thing is needful: and Mary hath chosen that good part, which shall not be taken away from her.

LUKE 10.38-42

Of the many words beginning with the letter 'H' – the positive ones like 'hope' and 'happiness' and 'heaven', or the negative ones like 'hatred', 'hypocrisy' and 'hell' – the one I have chosen for this chapter is 'hospitality'. Paul and Timothy both enjoin us 'to be given to hospitality' and the Gospels are full of examples of the way in which people of all sorts and conditions took pleasure in entertaining Jesus in their homes.

Perhaps the best known is that story of Martha and Mary, and it is impossible not to be torn in two in one's sympathy for Martha, slaving away in the kitchen in a cloud of steam and self-pity, and for Mary who for once was prepared to abandon domesticity for such a rare opportunity to sit alone at the feet of her Lord.

It's all very well
Sitting in the shade of the courtyard
Talking about your souls.
Someone's got to see to the cooking,
Standing at the oven all morning
With you two taking your ease.
It's all very well
Saying he'd be content
With bread and honey.
Perhaps he would – but I wouldn't,
Coming to our house like this,
Not giving him of our best,
Yes, it's all very well
Him trying to excuse you,
Saying your recipe's best,
Saying I worry too much,
That I'm always anxious.
Someone's got to worry –
And double if the others don't care.
For it's all very well
Talking of faith and belief,
But what would you do
If everyone sat in the cool
Not getting their meals?
And he can't go wandering and preaching
On an empty stomach –
He'd die in the first fortnight.
Then where would you be
With all your discussions and questions
And no one to answer them?
It's all very well.

CLIVE SANSOM *Mary of Bethany*

This conflict is resolved by St Teresa of Avila – whose teaching is so similar to our own Mother Teresa four hundred years later – in the advice which she gave to her nuns when she wrote:

> God does not conduct us all by the same way. It may chance that those who think themselves to be lower than all may be the most exalted in the eyes of the Lord; and though every soul . . . is called to prayer, it does not follow that all must be contemplatives.
> St Martha was holy, though we are not told that she was contemplative; and what more do you want than to become such as was this blessed woman, who deserved so often to entertain Christ, our Lord, and to give Him sustenance, to serve Him, and to eat at His table? If she had been like the Magdalene, rapt in contemplation, there would have been no-one to give to eat to this divine Guest . . . Remember, it is necessary that some-one should cook the food, and think yourselves happy in serving with Martha; recollect that true humility consists in being very ready to be satisfied with what the Lord wishes to make of us; and always to consider ourselves unworthy to be called His servants.
>
> ST TERESA OF AVILA *The Way of Perfection*

The 'retort courteous' which Jesus gives to Martha is matched by His sharper but equally compassionate rebuke when He accepts the hospitality of the wealthy Pharisee to come to a meal in his house.

As host the unfortunate man is acutely embarrassed by the intrusion of one of the local prostitutes.

> And behold, a woman in the city, which was a sinner, when she knew that Jesus sat at meat in the Pharisee's house, brought an alabaster box of ointment,
> And stood at his feet behind him weeping, and began to wash his feet with tears, and did wipe them with the hairs of her head and kissed his feet, and anointed them with the ointment.
>
> LUKE 7.37

But Jesus instantly sees the contrast between the spontaneous love and warmth of her hospitable gesture and the conventional hospitality of the Pharisee. Better a dinner of herbs where love is, than a stalled ox . . .

> And he turned to the woman, and said unto Simon, Seest thou this woman? I entered into thine house, thou gavest me no water for my feet: but she hath washed my feet with tears, and wiped them with the hairs of her head.
> Thou gavest me no kiss: but this woman since the time I came in, hath not ceased to kiss my feet.
> My head with oil thou didst not anoint: but this woman hath anointed my feet with ointment.
>
> LUKE 7.44-46

There is a poem by Gerard Manley Hopkins which sums up for me the full meaning of the word 'hospitality'; a poem in which he describes the welcome he is given by a family living in the lovely valley of the river Elwy in North Wales, the warmth of which fills him with a sense of his own inadequacy which only his God can dispel:

I remember a house where all were good
To me, God knows, deserving no such thing:
Comforting smell breathed at very entering,
Fetched fresh, as I suppose, off some sweet wood.
That cordial air made those kind people a hood
All over, as a bevy of eggs the mothering wing
Will, or mild nights the new morsels of spring:
Why, it seemed of course; seemed of right it should.
Lovely the woods, waters, meadows, combes, vales,
All the air things wear that build this world of Wales;
Only the inmate does not correspond:
God, lover of souls, swaying considerate scales,
Complete thy creature dear O where it fails,
Being mighty a master, being a father and fond.

GERARD MANLEY HOPKINS *In the Valley of the Elwy*

I

I will wash my hands in innocency O Lord; and so will I go to thine altar.
That I may show the voice of thanksgiving: and tell of all Thy wondrous works.

PSALM 26.6-7

Keep innocency and take heed unto the thing that is right: for that shall bring a man peace at the last.

PSALM 37.37

They brought children for him to lay his hands on them with prayer. The disciples scolded them for it, but Jesus said to them 'Let the children come to me; do not try to stop them; for the kingdom of Heaven belongs to these.'

MATTHEW 19.14

Heaven lies about us in our infancy!
Shades of the prison-house begin to close
  Upon the growing boy,
But he beholds the light, and whence it flows,
  He sees it in his joy;
The youth who daily farther from the east
  Must travel, still is nature's priest,
  And by the vision splendid
  Is on his way attended;
At length the man perceives it die away,
And fade into the light of common day.

WILLIAM WORDSWORTH from
Ode on Intimations of Immortality

For me the letter 'I' stands for innocence and its charmingly archaic variant, innocency. It is a gift that most young children have, and one that a few very rare and special people retain all their lives – people like Mother Teresa even when they have seen the very worst that mankind can do to destroy innocence.

There is no more touching 'state of innocence and bliss' than that of a contented, well-fed baby bubbling and chuckling to itself, greeting besotted admirers with a seraphic smile, kicking and gurgling until it falls into a sleep of perfect contentment.

For infants time is like a humming shell
Heard between sleep and sleep, wherein the shores
Foam-fringed, wind-fluted of the strange earth dwell
And the sea's cavernous hunger faintly roars.
It is the humming pole of summer lanes
Whose sound quivers like heat-haze endlessly
Over the corn, over the poppied plains –
An emanation from the earth or sky.
Faintly they hear, through the womb's lingering haze,
A rumour of that sea to which they are born:
They hear the ringing pole of summer days,
But need not know what hungers for the corn.
They are the lisping rushes in a stream –
Grace-notes of a profound, legato dream.

C DAY LEWIS from *O Dreams, O Destinations*

Once the more fortunate of our children retained a quality of innocence until the disturbances of puberty, but now they are exposed to what Thomas Traherne called 'the dirty devices of the world' as soon as their eyes can focus on a television screen.

But I suppose it's no good ranting on about violence and the media. Children love vicarious violence and one remembers the story by the incomparable 'Saki' called 'The Toys of Peace' in which a high-minded uncle, instead of giving his young nephews an eagerly awaited fort and boxes of lead soldiers, arrives for Christmas with sets of district councillors and local government officials and models of a municipal wash-house and the Manchester branch of the YWCA. They are received in stunned silence, but his hopes of inculcating a spirit of peace and goodwill towards all men are thwarted when, a little later, he finds the children totally absorbed in a fierce battle raging round the YWCA and its terrified inmates, a little red paint having transformed the worthy civilians into bloody warriors. Children will continue to machine-gun each other to death with hideous simulation and enormous enjoyment totally unaware of the real horrors of war.

Walter de la Mare was deeply aware of this and of the poignancy of the children who twice in his life-time played at soldiers as little boys and died in battle too soon as young men. He expressed it in a poem which he called 'Keep Innocency'.

Like an old battle, youth is wild
With bugle and spear, and counter cry,
Fanfare and drummery, yet a child
Dreaming of that sweet chivalry,
The piercing terror cannot see.

He, with a mild and serious eye,
Along the azure of the years,
Sees the sweet pomp sweep hurtling by;
But he sees not death's blood and tears,
Sees not the plunging of the spears.

And all the strident horror of
Horse and rider in red defeat
Is only music fine enough
To lull him into slumber sweet
In fields where ewe and lambkin bleat.

. . .

And when the wheeling rout is spent,
Though in the heaps of slain he lie;

Or lonely in his last content;
Quenchless shall burn in secrecy
The flame Death knows his victors by.

WALTER DE LA MARE *Keep Innocency*

Any sensitive parents are haunted by the inevitability of their children's transition from the innocence of childhood to their own self-awareness; and it is very difficult for them to make themselves believe that 'Love is proved in the letting go'. Or, as Tony Connor puts it,

Sometimes when they are asleep,
I stand by the beds looking
at those beautiful variations
of the sadly drooping
flesh on our bones. I long,
on such nights, for mastery
of their features; as though they
might benefit by magic
of my close care – protected
from the poison and decay
of time, and the stains that mock
clean intention . . .

Then I bend, and smooth back hair
from a hot forehead, or, maybe
stroke a cheek. Not reconciled
to the undoubted wearing
out and dirtying they
must suffer to die wise men,

or fools; but less troubled by
the futility of my fierce
prayers, and the proud but modest
gestures of fatherly
love I make as though by force
of habit over each bed.

TONY CONNOR from *In the Children's Room*

J

'J' is a cheerful letter suggesting jollity and jesting; jubilation and joy. I associate it with the summer solstice, that climax of the year before the long descent into autumn and winter; the time of all the high midsummer joys which are epitomised in the word June.

> Now June walks on the waters,
> And the cuckoo's last enchantment
> Passes from Olton pools.
> Now dawn comes to my window
> Breathing midsummer roses,
> And scythes are wet with dew.
> Is it not strange for ever
> That, bowered in this wonder,
> Man keeps a jealous heart?
> That June and the June waters,
> And birds and dawn-lit roses,
> Are gospels in the wind,
> Fading upon the deserts,
> Poor pilgrim revelations?
> Hist . . . over Olton pools!
>
> JOHN DRINKWATER *Olton Pools*

The word June probably derives from Juno, the Roman goddess who was the Queen of Heaven, the great guardian of all women and the special protector of marriage. Perhaps this accounts for the old and comforting superstition that a June marriage will be a particularly happy one.

Midsummer, time of golden views and hazes,
Advance in genial air,
Bring out your best for this charmed pair –
Let fly a flamingo dawn, throw open all your roses,
Crimson the day for them and start the dancing.

June-month fruits, yield up your delicate favours
Entrancing them, and be
Foretastes of ripe felicity:
Peach bloom and orange flower, ravish these happy lovers,
Sweeten the hour for them and start the dancing.

. . .

In well deep looks of love and soft-as-foam
Glances they plight their troth.
Midsummer stars, be kind to both
Through the warm dark when they shall come into their own,
Light your candles for them, start the dance.

C DAY LEWIS from *A Marriage Song*

The word joy recurs throughout the Bible – particularly in its religous connotation as 'the delight and satisfaction of the soul in its unions with God' – from that first moment described with such matchless imagery in the book of Job when 'He laid the foundations of the earth, when the morning stars sang together, and all the sons of God shouted for joy.' It is the delight and satisfaction which the Psalmist felt when he said 'Thou wilt show me the paths of life: in thy presence is fulness of joy; at thy right hand there are pleasures for evermore'. And of course St Paul put it second only to love in his list of the fruits of the spirit.

Joy and sorrow are the bright and dark colours which set each other off in the pattern of our life cycle – even at the very beginning of that cycle, before birth. St Luke tells us that when Elizabeth heard the Virgin Mary's astonishing salutation 'the babe leapt in her womb for joy'. And at its end he describes how the old man Simeon died joyfully when he saw Mary's child presented in the Temple and recognised him as the Messiah – the Light of the World.

In the Acts of the Apostles we read of Paul's suffering and persecution during his missionary journeys and yet, knowing the dangers ahead and the near certainty that, like Stephen, he would die a martyr's death for his beliefs, he was still able to say 'none of these things move me, neither count I my life dear unto myself, so that I might finish my course with joy'.

And so joy and sorrow are inextricably, and often, in human terms, inexplicably interwoven in the pattern of life. But when the dark strands of suffering seem to be too dominant we can find reassurance in some of Christ's farewell words to His disciples with which He sought to give them comfort and strength before His arrest.

> Ye shall be sorrowful, but your sorrow shall be turned into joy. A woman when she is in travail hath sorrow, because her hour is come: but as soon as she is delivered of the child, she remembereth no more the anguish, for joy that a man is born into the world. And ye now therefore have sorrow: but I will see you again, and your heart shall rejoice, and your joy no man taketh from you.
>
> JOHN 16.20-22

The quality of joy changes as we progress through life. The innocent, unthinking joys of childhood give way to the agonies and ecstasies of adolescence; and these are replaced by the deeper joys of our maturity. But as we grow older and joy seems more elusive, we reach 'the years that bring the philosophic mind' when we can look back without envy as Wordsworth did in his great ode.

We in thought will join your throng,
Ye that pipe and ye that play,
Ye that through your hearts today
Feel the gladness of the May!
What though the radiance which was once so bright
Be now for ever taken from my sight,
Though nothing can bring back the hour
Of splendour in the grass, of glory in the flower;
We will grieve not, rather find
Strength in what is left behind;
In the primal sympathy
Which having been must ever be;
In the soothing thoughts that spring
Out of human suffering;
In the faith that looks through death,
In years that bring the philosophic mind.

WILLIAM WORDSWORTH from
Ode on Intimations of Immortality

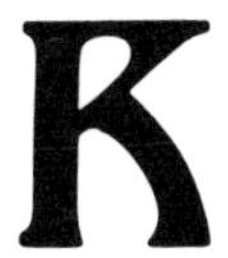

'Where the word of a king is, there is power, and who may say with him, what dost thou?'

ECCLESIASTES 8.4

'The Lord is our judge. The Lord is our law-giver. The Lord is our king. He will save us.'

ISAIAH 33.22

When it comes to the letter 'K' I see in my imagination a young child learning his letters by working through one of those illustrated Alphabets in which an outline of 'something beginning with "K"' is presented for him to colour. It may be a kitten or a kite, but most probably it will be a king sitting on a throne with a crown on his head.

And then he grows a little older and begins to learn about the kings of England:

Willie, Willie, Harry, Ste,
Harry, Dick, John, Harry three

And like most of us whose knowledge of history is as simplistic as that he will learn to distinguish between good kings and bad kings: bad kings who use their power to rule despotically, good kings who rule with justice and equity.

And when the young child starts to study the Bible, he will find that this holds good for the kings of Israel whose first king, Saul, used his power corruptly, but was succeeded by David, who became the greatest of them all. The special qualities of kingship which he brought to his task are summed up in the words of Isaiah.

The spirit of the Lord shall rest upon him, the spirit of wisdom and understanding, the spirit of counsel and might, the spirit of knowledge and of the fear of the Lord;
And shall make him of a quick understanding in the fear of the Lord: and he shall not judge after the sight of his eyes, neither reprove after the hearing of his ears:
But with righteousness shall he judge the poor, and reprove with equity for the meek of the earth:
And righteousness shall be the girdle of his loins, and faithfulness the girdle of his reins.

ISAIAH 11.2-5

The pathetic transience of 'might, majesty, dominion and power' in the worldly sense is brought home to us more poignantly in the death of kings than of lesser mortals and there is no more touching story in the Bible than the account of the last few days of King David's reign after all the adventurous early years – the triumph over Goliath, the long exile and bitter conflict with Saul, and his great welding of the people of Israel into a nation.

Now King David was old and stricken in years; and they covered him with clothes, but he gat no heat,
Wherefore his servants said unto him, Let there be sought for my Lord the king a young virgin; and let her stand before the king and let her cherish him, and let her lie in thy bosom, that my Lord the king may get heat.
So they sought for a fair damsel throughout all the coasts of Israel, and found Abishag a Shunammite, and brought her to the king.
And the damsel was very fair and cherished the king, and ministered to him, but the king knew her not.

I KINGS 1.1-4

In his farewell to Solomon – his son by his beloved Bathsheba – who was to succeed him on the throne David began with these words: 'I go the way of all the earth; be thou strong therefore and shew thyself a man.' And so the cycle of dominion and power was repeated.

'And king David said "Call me Zadok the priest" . . . and Zadok the priest took an horn of oil out of the tabernacle and anointed Solomon. And they blew the trumpet; and all the people said, God save king Solomon.'

I KINGS 1.32.39

And Solomon reigned for forty years in great splendour and wisdom until he too 'slept with his fathers' and was buried in the city of David, his father.

Some years ago the coffin of King Vasa the Second of Sweden was opened four hundred years after his death and royal burial. There is a macabre photograph of the open coffin showing the skull with its huge gaunt eye-sockets and gappy teeth, but still resting on the skull at a grotesquely jaunty angle is a small gold crown; and clasped in the bones of the right hand an elaborate sceptre.

The glories of our blood and state
Are shadows, not substantial things;
There is no armour against Fate;
Death lays his icy hand on kings:
Sceptre and crown
Must tumble down,
And in the dust be equal made
With the poor crooked scythe and spade.

Some men with swords may reap the field,
And plant fresh laurels where they kill;
But their strong nerves at last must yield;
They tame but one another still;
Early or late
They stoop to Fate,
And must give up their murmuring breath
When they, pale captives, creep to death.

The garlands wither on your brow;
Then boast no more your mighty deeds!
Upon Death's purple altar now
See where the victor-victim bleeds.
  Your heads must come
  To the cold tomb:
Only the actions of the just
Smell sweet and blossom in their dust.

JAMES SHIRLEY *Death the Leveller*

Through the long history of the kings of Israel – the good ones and the bad ones – the Jews always looked back on David as representing the kingly ideal – a man of action, yet a poet; a tender lover, yet a stern dispenser of justice; a generous foe and a loyal friend. And they waited down the centuries for their Messiah to appear in a similar but even more masterful role.

The qualities of kingship displayed by Jesus – 'great David's greater son' – who was heralded by John the Baptist as the Messiah were in sharp contrast to this exalted pattern. In the words of St Paul 'He made himself of no reputation and took upon him the form of a servant'.

Yet He was the immortal king who unloosed the grip of 'Death's icy hand' from both mortal kings and commoners and whose aspirations are summed up in those majestic words of the Book of Common Prayer;

O Lord our heavenly Father, high and mighty, King of kings, Lord of lords, the only ruler or princes, who dost from they throne behold all the dwellers upon earth: Most heartily we beseech thee with thy favour to behold our most gracious Sovereign Lady Queen Elizabeth; and so replenish her with the grace of thy Holy Spirit, that she may always incline to thy will, and walk in thy way: Endue her plenteously with heavenly gifts; grant her in health and wealth long to live; strengthen her that she may vanquish and overcome all her enemies, and, finally after this life she may attain everlasting joy and felicity; through Jesus Christ our Lord.

Godliness with contentment is great gain.
For we brought nothing into this world, and it is certain we can carry nothing out.
And having food and raiment let us be therewith content.
But they that will be rich fall into temptation and a snare, and into many foolish and hurtful lusts, which drown men in destruction and perdition.
For the love of money is the root of all evil:

1 TIMOTHY 6.6-10

Praise the Lord O my soul, and forget not all his benefits.
Who saveth thy life from destruction; and crowneth thee with mercy and loving kindness.
Who satisfieth thy mouth with good things, making thee young and lusty as an eagle.

PSALM 103.2-5

The letter 'L' immediately suggests light and where there is light there is life and laughter and loving-kindness. But it also suggests dark words like lament and lying and lechery and loathsomeness. Somewhere between the two are the rather equivocal words 'lust' and 'lusty'.

'Lusty' suggests vigour and enthusiasm and is a wholly admirable word; moreover one not only descriptive of youth. The faithful old servant, Adam, in *As You Like It* commends himself to Orlando by saying, 'Though I look old, yet I am strong and lusty'; and he adds a totally disarming bonus. 'My age is as a lusty winter, frosty but kindly'.

'Lust' on the other hand is one of those words that has come down in the world. It is derived from an Anglo-Saxon word, meaning delight, but has finished up as the fourth of the seven deadly sins.

It usually refers to the lusts of the flesh and as such comes in for some pretty rough handling in the Epistles with their ringing phrases about 'chambering and wantoning'. But no less selfish and deadly is the lust for money; and even deadlier, because it affects so many lives, is the ruthless lust for power: the monstrous egotism which is summed up with such economy of words in Walter de la Mare's poem describing Napoleon's reaction to the defeat of his army after Moscow.

> What is the world, O soldiers?
> It is I:
> I, this incessant snow,
>
> This northern sky;
> Soldiers, this solitude
> Through which we go
> Is I.
>
> WALTER DE LA MARE *Napoleon*

This equivocal nature of lust is dramatically illustrated in the story of King David and Bathsheba.

At the time when kings go forth to battle he has stayed on in Jerusalem while his army under the command of Joab is away fighting the Ammonites who are successfully holding out in the besieged town of Rabbah.

It is a hot night and sleep eludes the king as he lies thinking about how he is approaching middle age, how he is estranged from his wife; thinking too about his children, his people, his soliders.

> And it came to pass in an eveningtide, that David arose from off his bed, and walked upon the roof of the king's house: and from the roof he saw a woman washing herself; and the woman was very beautiful to look upon.
> And David sent and enquired after the woman. And one said,

Is not this Bathsheba, the daughter of Eliam, the wife of Uriah the Hittite?
And David sent messengers, and took her; and she came in unto him, and he lay with her, for she was purified from her uncleanness; and she returned unto her house.
And the woman conceived, and sent and told David, and said, I am with child.

II SAMUEL 11.2-5

Now Uriah of course was with the army; a brave but rather brainless professional soldier wedded more to warfare than to his wife. And it was not surprising that after what appeared to be a crude seduction Bathsheba fell in love with the king, but for a woman divorce was forbidden and adultery a mortal sin. Duff Cooper in his masterly reconstruction of the story sets out David's dilemma.

David himself found it difficult to believe that there could be great evil at the root of so much good. For he was happy as he had never been, having in one person the mistress whom he adored, the counsellor whom he respected, and the sweet companion of whom he was never weary. His relations with God were of so intimate and close a character that he could not feel happy if he thought that God was angry. Conversely, he could not believe that God was angry when he felt so supremely happy.

ALFRED DUFF COOPER *David*

Here are the ingredients of countless novels and in one by Rose Macaulay she restates this timeless dilemma when she writes of one of the characters:

And then I thought how *odd* it was, all that love and joy and peace that flooded over me when I thought about him and how it all came from what was a deep meanness in our loves, for that is what adultery is, a meanness and a stealing, a taking away from someone what should be theirs, a great selfishness, and surrounded and guarded by lies lest it should be found out. And out of this meanness and this selfishness and this lying flow love and joy and peace, beyond anything that can be imagined. And this makes a discord in the mind, the happiness and the guilt and the remorse pulling in opposite ways so that the mind and soul are torn in two, and if it goes on for years and years the discord becomes permanent, so that it will never stop, and even if one goes on living after death there will still be this deep discord that nothing can heal, because of the great meanness and selfishness that caused such a deep joy. And there is no way out of this dilemma that I know.

ROSE MACAULAY *The Towers of Trebizond*

Lust, anger, hatred are at least robust vices that can keep company with greatness. But the meanness and the selfishness and the lying and the cruelty to which David sinks to achieve his ends are despicable.

First he recalls Uriah from the front in the hope that he will appear to be the father. Unfortunately for David Uriah's strict code of military etiquette foils the plan.

But Uriah slept at the door of the king's house with all the servants of his lord, and went not down to his house. And when they had told David, saying, Uriah went not down unto his house, David said unto Uriah, Camest thou not from thy journey? why then didst thou not go down unto thine house? And Uriah said unto David, The Ark, and Israel, and Judah, abide in tents; and my lord Joab, and the servants of my lord, are encamped in the open fields; shall I then go into mine house, to eat and to drink, and to lie with my wife? As thou livest, and as thy soul liveth, I will not do this thing.

II SAMUEL 11.9-11

David then sinks still further and arranges for Uriah to take back a secret message to Joab. 'Set ye Uriah in the forefront of the hottest battle and retire ye from him that he may be smitten and die.' In due course Joab sends back the inevitable dispatch to his master from army headquarters.

I was near the king that day. I saw him snatch
And briskly scan the GHQ dispatch.
Thick-voiced he read it out. (His face was grave.)
'This officer advanced with the first wave,

'And when our first objective had been gained,
'(Though wounded twice), reorganised the line:
'The spirit of the troops was by his fine
'Example most effectively sustained.'

He gripped his beard; then closed his eyes and said,
'Bathsheba must be warned that he is dead.
'Send for her. I will be the first to tell
'This wife how her heroic husband fell.'

SIEGFRIED SASSOON *Devotion to Duty*

And so David achieves his object, but the dilemma remains unsolved. Are the means justified by the end, which was that Bathsheba loved and cherished him until he died in old age and bore him Solomon, one of the greatest of all the kings of Israel? God moves in a mysterious way his wonders to perform.

The days of our years are threescore years and ten; and if by reason of strength they be four score years, yet is their strength labour and sorrow; for it is soon cut off and we fly away.
So teach us to number our days, that we may apply our hearts unto wisdom.

PSALM 90.10, 12

The profit of life consists not in the space, but rather in the use. Some have lived long who have lived but a short while. Make use of life while you have it. Whether you have lived enough depends upon yourself, not on the number of your years. Did you imagine you would never arrive at the place towards which you were for ever moving? There is no road but hath an end. And, if company may solace you, doth not the whole world go the same way?

MONTAIGNE *Essays*

We are just half-way through this progression from A to Z, from Alpha to Omega, the first and the last. So it seems fitting, out of all the splendid emotive words beginning with 'M' – might, majesty, melancholy – to have chosen mortality. 'There is no road but hath an end' is inevitably one of the great recurring themes of literature, and especially of the poets, since man first became aware of his mortality.

Like to the grass that's newly sprung,
Or like a tale that's new begun,

Or like a bird that's here to-day,
Or like the pearled dew of May,
Or like an hour, or like a span,
Or like the singing of a swan,
E'en such is man; – who lives by breath,
Is here, now there, in life and death.
The grass withers, the tale is ended,
The bird is flown, the dew's ascended,
The hour is short, the span's not long,
The swan's near death – man's life is done!

SIMON WASTELL *Like to the grass*

I am haunted by another phrase from that essay by Montaigne. 'Some have lived long who have lived but a short while.' The death of the young men in the two world wars and the fighting that still goes on in so many parts of the world continues to haunt us; the feeling that we have failed them, that their sacrifice may have been in vain; that to apply the word 'glorious' to their deaths is a mockery – something which melancholy old A E Housman perhaps foresaw in one of his finest poems:

The lads in their hundreds to Ludlow come in for
the fair,
There's men from the barn and the forge and the
mill and the fold,
The lads for the girls and the lads for the liquor are
there,
And there with the rest are the lads that will never
be old.

There's chaps from the town and the field and the
till and the cart,
And many to count are the stalwart, and many the
brave,

And many the handsome of face and the handsome of heart,
And few that will carry their looks or their truth to the grave.
I wish one could know them, I wish there were tokens to tell
The fortunate fellows that now you can never discern;
And then one could talk with them friendly and wish them farewell
And watch them depart on the way that they will not return.

But now you may stare as you like and there's nothing to scan;
And brushing your elbow unguessed-at and not to be told
They carry back bright to the coiner the mintage of man,
The lads that will die in their glory and never be old.

A E HOUSMAN *A Shropshire Lad*

Speculation about 'some have lived long who have lived but a short while' can be taken further. Supposing that Rupert Brooke had not died of septicaemia on his way to Gallipoli, that Keats had been cured of his TB, that Shelley had not drowned, would age have wearied them and the years condemned?

One person who, as I see it, lived but a short while but lived long, and has been a close companion of mine for over forty years since his diaries were first published, is the Reverend Francis Kilvert. A delicate man, unfitted for our English winters, he died in his thirties, only a few weeks after his marriage.

In one of the most moving passages towards the end of the diary he has a premonition of his own early death as he walks in his garden at Bredwardine one magical morning of early spring.

9th March 1878

I went out for a little while on the terrace this morning and walked up and down on the sunny side of the house. After how many illnesses such as this have I taken my first convalescent walk on the sunny terrace and always at this time of year when the honeysuckle leaves were shooting green and the apricot blossoms were dawning and the daffodils in blow. But some day will come the last illness from which there will be no going out to enjoy the sweet sights and sounds of the earthly spring, the singing of the birds, the opening of the fruit blossoms, the budding dawn of green leaves, and the blowing of the March daffodils. May I then be prepared to enter into the everlasting spring and to walk among the birds and flowers of Paradise.

FRANCIS KILVERT

There is no more poignant setting for the outward manifestations of mortality than the sale room, where loved and cherished possessions which have been part of a happy household for untold years are torn by death from their homely surroundings and sold to the highest bidder.

Lot 96: a brass-rimmed ironwork fender.
It had stood guard for years, where it used to
belong,
Over the hearth of a couple who loved tenderly.
Now it will go for a song.

Night upon winter night, as she gossiped with him
Or was silent, he watched the talkative firelight
send
Its reflections twittering over that burnished rim
Like a language of world without end.

Death, which unclasped their hearts, dismantled
all.

The world they made is as if it had never been true –
That firelit bubble of warmth, serene, magical,
Ageless in form and hue.

Now there stands, dulled in an auction room,
This iron thing – a far too durable irony,

Reflecting never a ghost of the lives that illumed it,
No hint of the sacred fire.

This lot was part of their precious bond, almost
A property of its meaning. Here, in the litter
Washed up by death, values are re-assessed
At a nod from the highest bidder.

C DAY LEWIS *Lot 96*

'N' for nostalgia: 'Yearning for what is past or inaccessible; sentimental evocation of past happiness; homesickness.' That is the definition given in the Penguin English Dictionary and it's rather a good one because it distinguishes between the two contrasting images of nostalgia. Firstly there is the positive one, the sentimental evocation of past happiness which is a harmless, indeed salutary, exercise because it helps to keep happy memories of the past clear and vivid. And the negative one, the yearning for what is inaccessible, with its boring parrot-cry about 'the good old days' with which the old so often alienate the young.

But then there is the third meaning of homesickness which is really neither a negative nor a positive state just a deep sadness, a terrible ache which a child feels when it is sent away to boarding school, or a young person to some remote posting overseas, or a whole nation when it is sent into captivity, like the sixty-year exile of the Jews to Babylon.

The sentimental evocation of past happiness, usually the happiness of childhood before the shades of the prison house begin to close, is something which most of us indulge in. And no harm is done if our memories become increasingly selective as we grow older so that the summers always seemed sunny and cloudless, and in the winter there was always tobogganing and skating and sparkling frost. Where are the snows of yesteryear?

> I had almost forgotten the singing in the streets,
> Snow piled up by the houses, drifting

Underneath the door into the warm room,
Firelight, lamplight, the little lame cat
Dreaming in soft sleep on the hearth, mother
  dozing,
Waiting for Christmas to come, the boys and me
Trudging over blanket fields waving lanterns to the
  sky.
I had almost forgotten the smell, the feel of it all,
The coming back home, with girls laughing like
  stars,

Their cheeks holly berries, me kissing one,
Silent-tongued, soberly, by the long church wall;
Then back to the kitchen table, supper on the
  white cloth,
Cheese, bread, the home-made wine;
Symbols of the Night's joy, a holy feast.
And I wonder now, years gone, mother gone,
The boys and girls scattered, drifted away with the
  snow flakes
Lamplight done, firelight over,
If the sounds of our singing in the street are still
  there,
Those old times. still praising:
And now, a lifetime of Decembers away from it all,
A branch of remembering holly spears my cheeks,
And I think it may be so;
Yes, I believe it may be so.

LEONARD CLARK *Singing in the Streets*

This positive evocation of past happiness can fill us with a feeling of gratitude and can be a source of comfort and strength as we grow older.

But what about the negative 'yearning for what is past or inaccessible', which is a messy mixture of self-pity and self-delusion? Self-delusion that everything in the past was better than it is today, and the self-pity which is a drug sapping our resolve, so that like D H Lawrence in a haunting poem 'our manhood is cast down in the flood of remembrance'.

Softly, in the dusk, a woman is singing to me;
Taking me back down the vista of years, till I see
A child sitting under the piano, in the boom of the
  tingling strings
And pressing the small, poised feet of a mother
  who smiles as she sings.

In spite of myself, the insidious mastery of song
Betrays me back, till the heart of me weeps to
  belong
To the old Sunday evenings at home, with winter
  outside
And hymns in the cosy parlour, the tinkling piano
  our guide.

So now it is vain for the singer to burst into
  clamour
With the great black piano appassionato. The
  glamour
Of childish days is upon me, my manhood is cast
Down in the flood of remembrance, I weep like a
  child for the past.

D H LAWRENCE *Piano*

The love of home is one of our deepest emotions. It was homesickness that drove the prodigal son back to his father; it was the driving force which repeopled Israel with the remnants from the ghettos and prison camps after the last war; and it is the recurring theme of all exiles. Even Robert Browning, happily married and living in Italy and sustained by beakersful of the warm south, could feel this aching homesickness for England.

Oh, to be in England
Now that April's there,
And whoever wakes in England
Sees, some morning unaware,
That the lowest boughs and the brushwood sheaf
Round the elm-tree bole are in tiny leaf,
While the chaffinch sings on the orchard bough
In England – now!
And after April, when May follows,
And the whitethroat builds, and all the swallows!
Hark, where my blossomed pear-tree in the hedge
Leans to the field and scatters on the clover
Blossoms and dewdrops – at the bent spray's edge –
That's the wise thrush; he sings each song twice
over,
Lest you should think he never could recapture
The first fine careless rapture!
And though the fields look rough with hoary dew
All will be gay when noontide wakes anew
The buttercups, the little children's dower
– Far brighter than this gaudy melon-flower!

ROBERT BROWNING *Home Thoughts from Abroad*

There is, I suppose, a sort of reverse nostalgia in the sense of yearning for what appears inaccessible, not in the past but in the future. If it is merely a manifestation of the grass being greener it is negative. On the other hand it is a positive spur to achievement when it is directed towards the fulfilment of some spiritual longing, so well expressed by poor sin-racked William Cowper with his plea:

'O for a closer walk with God,
A calm and heavenly frame;
A light to shine upon the road;
That leads me to the Lamb!'

The letter 'O' is a circle, symbolising the shape of the world, the round 'O' in which we live. And 'O' is for the offerings which we make to God and to our fellow travellers until sooner or later, but inevitably, 'our little life is rounded with a sleep'.

Offerings of many sorts – thank-offerings, love-offerings, sacrificial offerings – but firstly the basic thank-offering to God for our daily bread.

It is rather sad that, as a general rule, grace is no longer said before meals as part of the pattern of our domestic life, in which we offer thanks for the food which we are about to eat. Better, on the other hand, no grace at all than a mumbled, and for most people meaningless, 'Benedictus, Benedicat'; or worse still the guzzling 'gadarene' rush of 'For - what -we - are - about - to - receive - may - the - Lord - make - us - truly - thankful - Amen.'

I think my favourite grace, espcially on a sharp winter's morning before breakfast, is that enchantingly simple one with the curious line about 'cold as paddocks though they be', meaning cold as the skin of a toad.

> Here, a little child, I stand,
> Heaving up my either hand;
> Cold as paddocks though they be,
> Here I lift them up to Thee,
> For a benison to fall
> On our meat and on us all.
>
> ROBERT HERRICK *Grace For a Child*

There is an even older Elizabethan grace which we still use in our family for festive occasions. It is all-embracing in its prayer for, and thanks for, nourishing food, not only for the body but also for the spirit; and also for the loyal toast which the author offered to his earthly sovereign and which we can echo so aptly to her namesake today.

God bless our meat,
God guide our ways,
God give us grace
Our Lord to please.
Lord, long preserve in peace and health
Our gracious Queen Elizabeth.

GEORGE BELL OF EXETER

To offer thanks to God for our daily sustenence is our duty. To offer gifts as symbols of our gratitude should be our pleasure. And it doesn't matter how simple they are, provided that they are from the heart – like the precious gift which the woman of Bethany made to Christ.

Now when Jesus was in Bethany, in the house of Simon the leper,
There came unto him a woman having an alabaster box of very precious ointment, and poured it on his head, as he sat at meat.
But when his disciples saw it, they had indignation, saying, To what purpose is this waste?
For this ointment might have been sold for much, and given to the poor.
When Jesus understood it, he said unto them, Why trouble ye the woman? for she hath wrought a good work upon me.

MATTHEW 26.6-10

In contrast there is something rather repellant about the vulgar baggage-train with which the Queen of Sheba arrived on her visit to King Solomon and which was clearly designed to impress him, and strengthen her hand in negotiating a favourable trade-deal with him.

> And when the Queen of Sheba heard of the fame of Solomon, she came . . . to Jerusalem with a very great company, and camels that bare spices, and gold in abundance, and precious stones. And she gave the king an hundred and twenty talents of gold, and of spices great abundance, and precious stones; neither was there any such spice as the Queen of Sheba gave Solomon.
>
> 1 KINGS 10

The legend of the three wise men tells us that they brought offerings to lay at the feet of the Christ child. And painters have always depicted these as being contained in elaborately-wrought jewelled caskets which seem strangely out of place in the starkly simple surroundings of the stable in Bethlehem; to our eyes rather absurd encumbrances for the little family's flight into Egypt to escape from Herod's military police.

But however inappropriate the wise men's gifts may seem and however late they were in arriving on the scene after their arduous star-guided journey they brought with them offerings of love.

> The shepherds were here long before; even the cattle. They had joined the chorus of angels before you were on your way. For you the primordial discipline of the heavens was relaxed and a new defiant light blazed amid the disconcerted stars. How laboriously you came, taking sights and calculating, where the shepherds had run barefoot! How odd you looked on the road, attended by what outlandish liveries, laden with such preposterous gifts!
>
> Yet you came, and were not turned away. You too found room before the manger. Your gifts were not needed, but they were accepted and put carefully by, for they were brought with love.
>
> EVELYN WAUGH *Helena*

The wise men brought three symbolic offerings; gold is the symbol of a king, frankincense of a priest, and myrrh of suffering and sacrifice; and it was this gift which foreshadowed Christ's sacrifice upon the cross for the sins of the whole world. An event which was foreshadowed in its turn by one of the most haunting incidents in the Old Testament when God commands Abraham to sacrifice his only son Isaac, with its cruel cat and mouse element so alien to our concept of a loving God.

> And Abraham stretched forth his hand, and took the knife to slay his son.
> And the angel of the Lord called unto him out of heaven, and said, Abraham, Abraham: and he said, Here am I.
> And he said, Lay not thine hand upon the lad, neither do thou any thing unto him: for now I know that thou fearest God, seeing thou hast not withheld thy son, thine only son from me.
> And Abraham lifted up his eyes, and looked, and behold behind him a ram caught in a thicket by his horns: and Abraham went and took the ram, and offered him up for a burnt offering in the stead of his son.
>
> GENESIS 22.10-13

In one of his most powerful war poems Wilfred Owen re-tells the story but this time the terrible sacrifice was demanded, the sacrificial offering of all those young men of the First World War ('half the seed of Europe') who died too soon.

> So Abram rose, and clave the wood, and went,
> And took the fire with him, and a knife.
> And as they sojourned both of them together,
> Isaac the first-born spake and said, My Father,
> Behold the preparations, fire and iron,
> But where the lamb for this burnt-offering?
> Then Abram bound the youth with belts and
> straps,

And builded parapets and trenches there,
And stretched forth the knife to slay his son.
When lo! an angel called him out of heaven,
Saying, Lay not thy hand upon the lad,
Neither do anything to him. Behold,
A ram, caught in a thicket by its horns;
Offer the ram of pride instead of him.
But the old man would not so, but slew his son –
And half the seed of Europe, one by one.

WILFRED OWEN *The Parable of the Old Men and the Young*

The letter 'P' releases a quiverful of splendidly emotive arrow words – praise, providence, prayer, penitence, protection, peace – and how convenient for our Alphabet that they all find their deepest expression in the book of Psalms. This book which Martin Luther called 'a Bible in miniature' consists of 150 poems intended to be sung, which mirror all the spiritual experiences of the human soul and which transcend all our doctrinal differences.

The Psalms were central to the life and teaching of Christ who quoted them on the Cross and died with their words on His lips. They were the inspiration of the early apostles in their time of persecution, and they have remained at the heart of the worship of the Christian Church right up to the present day as the basis of its prayers and hymns.

There are many recurring themes, one of the dominant ones being God's protection, His foreseeing care which is so vividly summed up in that marvellous mixed metaphor.

> He shall cover thee with his feathers, and under his wings shalt thou trust; his truth shall be thy shield and buckler.
>
> PSALM 91

Then there are the Psalms of penitence, of supplication in which the writer seeks to find relief from the black depth of depression engendered by the catalogue of shortcomings which his self-examination has revealed.

> Out of the depths have I cried unto thee, O Lord.

> Lord, hear my voice: let thine ears be attentive to the voice of my supplications.
>
> If thou, Lord, shouldest mark iniquities, O Lord, who shall stand?
> But there is forgiveness with thee, that thou mayest be feared.
> I wait for the Lord, my soul doth wait, and in his word do I hope.
> My soul waiteth for the Lord more than they that watch for the morning: I say, more than they that watch for the morning.
> Let Israel hope in the Lord: for with the Lord there is mercy, and with him is plenteous redemption.
>
> PSALM 130. 1-7

Another recurring theme is the Psalmist's thanksgiving for God's providence, for the natural order and for man's place in it, in which the language of the Authorised Version achieves its highest poetry:

> He sendeth the springs into the valleys, which run among the hills.
> They give drink to every beast of the field: the wild asses quench their thirst.
> By them shall the fowls of the heaven have their habitation, which sing among the branches.
> He causeth the grass to grow for the cattle, and herb for the service of man: that he may bring forth food out of the earth;
> And wine that maketh glad the heart of man, and oil to make his face to shine, and bread which strengtheneth man's heart.
> Man goeth forth unto his work and to his labour until the evening.
> O Lord, how manifold are thy works! in wisdom hast thou made them all: the earth is full of thy riches.
>
> PSALM 104. 10-15, 23, 24

But the over-riding theme is worship and praise – the attempt to express in words a confession of faith in the 'might, majesty, dominion and power' of God the creator.

Like the closing bars of some great symphony the last six Psalms devote themselves solely to this theme so that they end with all the instruments of the orchestra – trumpets, lutes, harps, cymbals, stringed instruments and pipes blazing forth the last all-embracing verse. 'Let everything that hath breath praise the Lord. Praise ye the Lord.'

The best-known and most loved of all the Psalms must surely be the twenty-third which combines in six matchless verses all the ingredients of praise and thanksgiving, protection and providence, comfort and guidance.

Many of the Psalms have been adapted as hymns: 'As pants the hart for cooling streams', 'O God, our help in ages past' and so on, but none has inspired such a wealth of variations as 'The Lord is my Shepherd'. The universality of its appeal is well illustrated in the metrical version of the words by the English Nonconformist, Isaac Watts, when they are set to a hymn tune from the southern States of America based on a traditional Irish melody.

My Shepherd will supply my need,
Jehovah is his name;
In pastures fresh he makes me feed
Beside the living stream.

He brings my wand'ring spirit back
When I forsake his ways,
He leads me for his mercy's sake
In paths of truth and grace.

When I walk through the shades of death
Thy presence is my stay;
One word of thy supporting breath
Drives all my fears away.

Thy hand, in sight of all my foes
Doth still my table spread;
My cup with blessings overflows,
Thy oil anoints my head.

The sure provisions of my God
Attend me all my days;
O may thy house be my abode
And all thy works my praise.

There would I find a settled rest,
Where others go and come;
No more a stranger or a guest,
But like a child at home.

ISAAC WATTS *Psalm 23*

Better is an handful with quietness, than both the hands full with travail and vexation of spirit.

ECCLESIASTES 4.6

Better is a dry morsel and quietness therewith, than a house full of sacrifices with strife.

PROVERBS 17.1

The work of righteousness shall be peace; and the effect of righteousness quietness and assurance for ever.

ISAIAH 32.17

The letter 'Q' for quiet, and quietness and that most soothing of words quietude. And of course 'Q' is for Quakers, the Society of Friends, whose religious practice is the essence of quietude; an essence so perfectly distilled by the Quaker poet, John Greenleaf Whittier, in words from one of his hymns:

O sabbath rest by Galilee!
O calm of hills above,
Where Jesus knelt to share with thee
The silence of eternity,
Interpreted by love!

It is not easy to find quietude today when the isle is full of noises of cars and lorries and aircraft and transistors and all the other jarring sounds of our modern urban life which assault and hurt the ear as well as the soul.

When Christ needed to get away from the clamour of the crowds He went up into a mountain to pray; and thank God there are still mountains and hills and stretches of countryside where many people still find it possible to achieve quietude and a mood of calmness.

> . . . that blessed mood
> In which the burthen of the mystery,
> In which the heavy and the weary weight
> Of all this unintelligible world,
> Is lightened; that serene and blessed mood,
> In which the affections gently lead us on –
> Until, the breath of this corporeal frame
> And even the motion of our human blood
> Almost suspended, we are laid asleep
> In body, and become a living soul:
> While with an eye made quiet by the power
> Of harmony, and the deep power of joy,
> We see into the life of things.

WILLIAM WORDSWORTH from
Lines Written Above Tintern Abbey

In such surroundings we tend to look back nostalgically to the long peace and quietude of Victorian England – 'a land in which it seemed always afternoon'. And we forget the horrors of the industrial revolution, the slums, the gin palaces, the child prostitution, the dirt and the disease; and after the Franco-Prussian war the haunting prospect of greater wars to come. Gerard Manley Hopkins, who felt the conflicting pulls of poetry and the priesthood, worked for a time as an assistant priest in the slums of Liverpool where he saw all these things; and at this time (just on a hundred years ago) he wrote a poem about peace of mind, about the need for quietude which he likened to the shy, restless elusive wood-dove before it finally makes its nest and starts to brood and sit.

> When will you ever, Peace, wild wood-dove, shy wings shut,
> Your round me roaming end, and under be my boughs?
> When, when, Peace, will you, Peace? I'll not play hypocrite
> To my own heart: I yield you do come sometimes; but
> That piecemeal peace is poor peace. What pure peace allows
> Alarms of wars, the daunting wars, the death of it?
> O surely, reaving Peace, my Lord should leave in lieu
> Some good! And so he does leave Patience exquisite,
> That plumes to Peace thereafter. And when Peace here does house
> He comes with work to do, he does not come to coo,
> He comes to brood and sit.

GERARD MANLEY HOPKINS *Peace*

I suppose it can be said that Gerard Manley Hopkins' brilliant intellect and command of language was lost on those children of the industrial revolution under his charge, yet had he spent his whole life in some cloistered quietude he would not have experienced the agony of spirit which produced his finest poetry.

All priests are not poets but in the long history of the Christian Church there have always been faithful men who have tried to preach words of hope and comfort so that their flock could serve God with a quiet mind. R S Thomas, himself a priest, described them with marvellous understanding.

I see them working in old rectories
By the sun's light, by candle-light,
Venerable men, their black cloth
A little dusty, a little green
With holy mildew. And yet their skulls,
Ripening over so many prayers
Toppled into the same grave
With oafs and yokels. They left no books,
Memorial to their lonely thought
In grey parishes; rather they wrote
On men's hearts and in the minds
Of young children sublime words
Too soon forgotton. God in his time
Or out of it will correct this.

R S THOMAS *The Country Clergy*

One such priest who has long been forgotten was Augustus William Hare, a man of wealth, educated at Winchester and Oxford and with the promise of a brilliant academic career. But because of ill-health and the need to live in the country he was appointed in 1829 to the living of Alton Priors, a small parish in Wiltshire which consisted of a few cottages clustered about a tiny Saxon church. And there he set out with great humility to prepare his sermons for the handful of simple country people who formed his congregation: sermons which they could understand and which would help them in their daily living. As one of them said, 'Mr Hare, he do *long* to save our souls.'

He died of TB in 1834 and two years later his 'Sermons to a Country Congregation' were published. I came across a copy the other day and among them was a sermon on quietude which contained these 'sublime words too soon forgotten':

> Have any of you happened to see the effect of a breeze on a pool of deep water in a sheltered valley? The wind may be sharp enough to ruffle the face of the water for a while; but its depths are at peace. So is it with the Christian. The cares and worries

of life cannot pierce below the surface of his spirit: for he is lying beneath the shelter of his Saviour; and so the depths of his heart are safe from every common trouble and annoyance. Nothing earthly can shake his soul, unless it be one of those heavy storms and whirlwinds of affliction, with which it sometimes pleases God to try the patience of his servants. But God never tasks his children beyond their power. Apart however from these heavy heartsearching woes, which befall us, God be praised, very rarely, the Christian enjoys great peace. To a mind like his, a mind at ease in itself, and feeding on the promises of its God and Saviour, what matter those outward grievances and distresses, which harass and trouble the children of this world? Truly they are little more to him, than the rattling of the hail on the tiles to a man sitting by a good fire with a plentiful meal before him.

A W HARE *Sermons to a Country Congregation*

Who in the heavens can be compared with the Lord? Who among the sons of the mighty can be likened unto the Lord? God is greatly to be feared in the assembly of the saints, and to be had in reverence of all that are about him.

PSALM 89.6-7

Honour all men. Love the brotherhood. Fear God. Honour the king.

1 PETER 2.17

For every beast that walketh the earth and every bird that flieth with wings is a people like to ourselves. From the Lord they come; to the Lord they shall return.

THE KORAN

'R' is for reverence – a majestic word with a whole range of meanings as illustrated in those three quotations. Firstly its meaning of awe before the presence of some higher being; secondly respect for our fellow-men and for those who hold justifiable authority. And finally, in those words from the Koran, a concern for all living creatures, all the works of nature, which is summed up in the phrase 'reverence for life' – first coined by that great and good man Dr Albert Schweitzer. We try to express our reverence for God in many ways; in our words and music, in our works of art and in our buildings – whether they are as austere as some remote hermit's cell or as sublime as Salisbury Cathedral with its spire reaching to the sky.

In our world of advanced technology we are at last beginning to realise that reverence for life is not just a sentimental dream, that we can no longer afford to exploit the world's dwindling resources indefinitely or destroy the balance of nature. And with our ever increasing urbanisation we also destroy the ancient beauty of our countryside. This unthinking and irrevocable destruction is nowhere more forcibly condemned than in Gerard Manley Hopkins' poem 'Binsey Poplars'. One March afternoon in 1879, when he was living in Oxford, he walked along the river Thames up-stream to Godstow and was shattered to find that a row of aspens which lined the bank had all been felled.

My aspens dear, whose airy cages quelled,
Quelled or quenched in leaves the leaping sun,
All felled, felled, are all felled;
Of a fresh and following golden rank
Not spared, not one
That dandled a sandalled
Shadow that swam or sank
On meadow and river and wind-wandering
weed-winding bank.

O if we but knew what we do
When we delve or hew –
Hack and rack the growing green!
Since country is so tender
To touch, her being so slender,
That, like this sleek and seeing ball
But a prick will make no eye at all,
Where we, even where we mean
To mend her we end her,
When we hew or delve:
After-comers cannot guess the beauty been.
Ten or twelve, only ten or twelve
Strokes of havoc unselve
The sweet especial scene,
Rural scene, a rural scene,
Sweet especial rural scene.

GERARD MANLEY HOPKINS *Binsey Poplars*

Our dealings with the world of wild creatures have been, with honourable exceptions, pretty shoddy. Consideration for animals was an aspect of Christian charity which the early Church largely ignored despite Christ's all-embracing compassion.

Even today our exploitation of the animal world, though checked spasmodically by legislation rather than by love, is still all too painfully manifest and we still hold to the arrogant belief that as superior beings all animals are our property. There is an Apocryphal story, but it bears the ring of truth, which illustrates Christ's practical example in this matter.

> It happened that the Lord went forth from the city and walked with his disciples over the mountains. And they came to a mountain, and the road which led to it was steep. There they found a man with a sumpter-mule. But the animal had fallen, for the burden was too heavy, and he beat it that it bled. And Jesus came to him and said, Man, why dost thou beat thine animal? Seest thou not that it is too weak for its burden, and knowest thou not that it suffers pains? But the man answered and said, What is that to you? I can beat it as much as I please, since it is my property, and I bought it for a good sum of money. Ask those that are with thee, for they know and know thereof. And some of the disciples said, Yea Lord, it is as he says. We have seen how he bought it. But the Lord said, Do you not notice how it bleeds, and hear you not how it laments and cries? But they answered and said, Nay Lord, we hear not how it laments and cries. And the Lord was sad and exclaimed, Woe to you, that hear not how it complains to the Creator in heaven, and cries for mercy. But three times woe to him of whom it complains and cries in its distress. And he came forth and touched the animal. And it arose and its wounds were healed. And Jesus said to the man, Now go on and beat it no more, that you also may find mercy.
>
> ST THOMAS'S GOSPEL

Despite the vast extension of our knowledge of life and natural phenomena the ocean of truth remains largely unplumbed and we would be wise to admit our ignorance. Job had no answer when

God asked him, 'Where wast *thou*, when I laid the foundations of the earth?' And with the humility of a true poet Robert Frost ponders the meaning of the life force and his reverence for it – even in its humblest form – in one of his poems.

A speck that would have been beneath my sight
On any but a paper sheet so white
Set off across what I had written there.
And I had idly poised my pen in air
To stop it with a period of ink
When something strange about it made me think.
This was no dust speck by my breathing blown,
But unmistakably a living mite
With inclinations it could call its own.
It paused as with suspicion of my pen,
And then came racing wildly on again
To where my manuscript was not yet dry;
Then paused again and either drank or smelt
With loathing, for again it turned to fly.
Plainly with an intelligence I dealt.
It seemed too tiny to have room for feet,
Yet must have had a set of them complete
To express how much it didn't want to die.
It ran with terror and with cunning crept.
It faltered; I could see it hesitate;
Then in the middle of the open sheet
Cower down in desperation to accept
Whatever I accorded it of fate . . .

Since it was nothing I knew evil of
I let it lie there till I hope it slept.

I have a mind myself and recognise
Mind when I meet with it in any guise.
No one can know how glad I am to find
On any sheet the least display of mind.

ROBERT FROST *A Considerable Speck*

The law of the Lord is perfect, converting the soul;
The testimony of the Lord is sure, making wise the simple.

PSALM 19.7

The Lord preserveth the simple; I was brought low and He helped me.

PSALM 116.6

Charles Wesley wrote many splendid hymns. Not only the exultant Sunday ones like 'O for a thousand tongues to sing' and 'Lo He comes with clouds descending', but the bracing Monday ones as well 'Forth in Thy Name O Lord I go, my daily labour to pursue'. But even as a not particularly manly child I was never very happy with what must be his best known hymn of all:

Gentle Jesus meek and mild,
Look upon a little child,
Pity my simplicity,
Suffer me to come to Thee.

One just wasn't happy about that spineless first line. At no time in His earthly life could Christ have been called meek and mild; taking on His elders and betters in argument in the temple at the age of twelve; casting out the money-changers; courageous and dignified throughout His political trial. But not meek and mild.

On the other hand I'm all for simplicity, 'S' for 'simplicity', whatever age you are and it is an attribute to be thankful for, not pitied.

The behavioural scientists and sociologists and in-depth interviewers who try to sort us out too often only seem to complicate our lives with their jargon and God must surely pity their complexity. It is a relief to turn for comfort to the cool economy of words used by Emily Dickinson.

How happy is the little stone
That rambles in the road alone,
And doesn't care about careers,
And exigencies never fears;
Whose coat of elemental brown
A passing universe put on;
And independent as the sun,
Associates or glows alone,
Fulfilling absolute decree
In casual simplicity.

EMILY DICKINSON *How Happy is the Little Stone*

Of course it's all right for little stones. But unfortunately most of us have to care about careers and are afraid of exigencies, and life is too complicated to be lived in casual simplicity. It is difficult enough to understand our own motives, but almost impossible to fathom those of other people.

That still neglected poet, John Tessimond, whose permutated love life was so constantly going astray, summed it up quite simply:

One day people will touch and talk perhaps easily,
And loving be natural as breathing and warm as
sunlight,
And people will untie themselves, as string is
unknotted,
Unfold and yawn and stretch and spread their
fingers,
Unfurl, uncurl like seaweed returned to the sea,
And work will be simple and swift as a seagull
flying,

And play will be casual and quiet as a seagull
settling,
And the clocks will stop, and no-one will wonder
or care or notice,
And people will smile without reason, even in the
winter, even in the rain.

A S J TESSIMOND *Daydream*

In addition to the word 'simplicity', the sibilant letter 'S', more than any other letter in the alphabet, conjures up in the mind peaceful associations – serenity, sleep, starlight, spindrift, summer skies; scenes like those two magical ones in *Wuthering Heights* which strike like a shaft of sunlight through the lowering clouds of that sombre novel.

He said the pleasantest manner of spending a hot July day was lying from morning till evening on a bank of heath in the middle of the moors, with the bees humming dreamily about among the bloom, and the larks singing high up overhead, and the blue sky and bright sun shining steadily and cloudlessly. That was his most perfect idea of heaven's happiness; mine was rocking in a rustling green tree, with a west wind blowing, and bright white clouds flitting rapidly above: and not only larks, but throstles, and blackbirds and linnets, and cuckoos pouring out music on every side, and the moors seen at a distance, broken into cool dusky dells, but close by great swells of long grass undulating in waves to the breeze.

EMILY BRONTE *Wuthering Heights*

And so to the definitive word beginning with S – silence. Silence in all its forms; from the cold silence of unspoken hostility to the close silence of two minds in absolute accord, or the elected silence of the cloistered nun in Gerard Manley Hopkins' poem who is out of the swing of our tempestuous sea.

I have desired to go
Where springs not fail,

To fields where flies no sharp and sided hail
  And a few lilies blow.

And I have asked to be
  Where no storms come,
Where the green swell is in the havens dumb,
  And out of the swing of the sea.

GERARD MANLEY HOPKINS *Heaven-Haven*

It is comforting to know that there are still places where men and women live out their lives in simple devotion to God and in praying for the world. A thousand years in Thy sight are as but a watch in the night. So their prayer is part of the eternal stream of worship which has gone up to God since man became a conscious soul.

It is part of the same stream which went up from the great medieval foundations which were destroyed at the Dissolution.

And if you wander on a still silent autumn afternoon round the bare ruined choirs of Fountains or Rievaulx or Glastonbury you begin to understand, however dimly, the meaning of time and eternity:

There, syllabled by silence, let me hear
The still, small voice which reached the prophet's
  ear.

. . .

There let me strive with each besetting sin,
Recall my wandering fancies, and restrain
The sore disquiet of a restless brain;
And, as the path of duty is made plain,
May grace be given that I may walk therein.

J G WHITTIER from *First-day Thoughts*

T

These Things have I spoken unto you that in me ye might have peace; in the world ye shall have tribulation: but be of good cheer. I have overcome the world.

JOHN 16.33

We glory in tribulations also; knowing that tribulation worketh patience; and patience experience; and experience hope.

ROMANS 5.3-4

Two words beginning with 'T' – two sharply contrasted yet complimentary words – will always be associated in my mind with the Battle of Britain. 'T' is for tribulation and 'T' is for triumph. The dictionary definition of that robust and rather old-fashioned word, tribulation, is brief and dispiriting. It merely defines it as 'affliction, distress, suffering.' The New Bible Dictionary on the other hand is more positive when it says:

> The English word is derived from the Latin tribulum, the threshing instrument or harrow by means of which the Roman husbandman separated the corn from the husks. Though tribulation may crush and bruise us, it separates our chaff from the wheat, so that we are prepared for the granary of heaven.

It is more than forty years since Munich which gave us that brief respite before the inevitable confrontation with a re-armed Germany. No one in his senses doubted that before long we should have to go through great tribulation, but only the faint-hearted doubted our ultimate triumph; few foresaw that the decisive battle would be fought two years later by a handful of young men in the September skies.

Now it is a part of history, 'of old, unhappy, far-off things, and battles long ago.' And all we can do is to remember with thanksgiving their tribulation and their triumph.

> See how these names are fêted by the waving grass
> And by the streamers of white cloud
> And whispers of wind in the listening sky.
> The names of those who in their lives fought for life,
> Who wore at their hearts the fire's centre.
> Born of the sun they travelled a short while towards the sun,
> And left the vivid air signed with their honour.
>
> STEPHEN SPENDER from *I Think Continually of Those Who Were Truly Great*

Tribulation and triumph are part of the pattern of all life. The design is at its boldest when life is lived at the heroic heights of aerial combat, or when it is seen in the lives of men and women of larger mould like Mother Teresa, and Steve Biko and Solzhenitsyn. But it is no less distinct in the young soldier in the back streets of Belfast, or the poor forgotten prisoner of conscience who suffers heaven knows what tribulations and yet triumphs over his persecutors.

In the writings of Edward Thomas who was killed in the First World War, his relationship with his wife Helen is a recurring theme. In a passage from her autobiography she shows how she learnt to accept in their marriage the pattern of tribulation and triumph, of agony and ecstasy; the contrasting colours without which life becomes mere existence, a drab monochrome – 'no cross, no crown'.

> As I grew older I came to realise that everything that is a part of life is inevitable to it and must therefore be good. I could not be borne high upon the crest of ecstasy and joy unless I also knew the dreadful depths of the trough of the great waves of life. I could not be irridiated by such love without being swept by the shadow of despair. The rich teeming earth from which

all beauty comes is fed with decay; out of the sweat and labour of men grows the corn. We are born to die; if death were not, life would not be either. Pain and weakness and evil, as well as strength and passion and health, are part of the beautiful pattern of life, and as I grew up I learned that life is richer and fuller and finer the more you can understand not only in your brain and intellect but in your very being, that you must accept it all; without bitterness the agony, without complacency the joy.

HELEN THOMAS *World Without End*

The cry of earth's anguish went up unto God,
Lord, take away Pain!
The shadow that darkens the world Thou hast made;
The close coiling chain
That strangles the heart; the burden that weighs
On the wings that would soar.
Lord take away pain from the world thou has made,
That it love Thee the more.

Then answered the Lord to the world He had made
Shall I take away pain;
And with it the power of the soul to endure,
Made strong by the strain?
Shall I take away pity, that knits heart to heart,
And sacrifice high?
Will you lose all your heroes that lift from the flame
White brows to the sky?
Shall I take away love that redeems with a price?
And smiles through the loss?
Can ye spare from the lives that would climb unto mine
The Christ on His Cross?

C L DRAWBRIDGE *Thy Cry of Earth's Anguish Went Up to God*

The contrasts of darkness and light are seen at their most vivid in the trial and crucifixion and resurrection of Christ; the darkness of Good Friday and the brilliant dawn light at the empty tomb. And ever since, men and women in their moments of darkness have been upheld by that Light – the true Light which lighteth every man that cometh into the world.

It lit the darkness of the prison cell in which Dietrich Bonhoeffer was shut up for so long and from which he was taken to be hanged because of his heroic courage in combatting the same evil which our pilots had fought in the autumn of 1940.

A prayer he wrote during Christmas 1943, not only for himself but for all his fellow prisoners, finds an echo today:

Lord Jesus Christ,
You were poor
and in distress, a captive and forsaken as I am.
You know all man's troubles;
You abide with me
when all men fail me;
You remember and seek me;
It is your will that I should know you and turn to you.
Lord, I hear your call and follow;
Help me . . .

. . .

Lord, whatever this day may bring,
Your name be praised.
O God, be gracious to me and help me.
Give me strength to bear what you send,
and do not let fear rule over me;
I trust in your grace
and commit my life wholly into your hands.
Do with me according to your will
and as is best for me.
Whether I live or die, I am with you,
and you, my God, are with me.
Lord, I wait for your salvation
and for your kingdom.

DIETRICH BONHOEFFER from *Prayer for His Fellow Prisoners, Christmas 1943*

'U' is for union and unity and they are words which have particularly satisfying connotations. 'Behold how good and pleasant it is for brethren to dwell together in unity', says the Psalmist. Paul writing from prison to his friends in Ephasus urged them to keep the unity in the bond of peace. And the vision of St Francis was to dwell in unity not only with his brethren but with the whole of creation – his brother the sun, his sister the moon. Few of us would aspire to such an all-embracing sense of unity, but in our more ordinary lives we are constantly reminded – whether in the flesh or on television – of the unity which exists between, say, a rider and a horse, a blind man and his guide dog, a shepherd and his sheep-dog.

> Have you ever watched a sheep-dog at work? He is not an emotional animal. He goes on with his job quite steadily; takes no notice of bad weather, rough ground or of his own comfort. He seldom or never stops to be stroked. Yet his faithfulness and intimate communion with his master are one of the loveliest things in the world. Now and then he looks at the shepherd. And when the time comes for rest, they are generally to be found together.
>
> EVELYN UNDERHILL *The Light of Christ*

There is no less a sense of unity between ourselves and the inanimate – a potter with his wheel, a musician with his instrument, a cook with her kitchen utensils.

In one of his most perceptive poems C Day Lewis senses this feeling of unity at two very different intellectual levels – a man totally absorbed in playing Bach on his harpsichord, and a girl absorbed in the more mundane, but perhaps no less honourable, task of laying the fire which is to keep him warm.

I remember, as if it were yesterday,
Watching that girl from the village lay
The fire in a room where sunlight poured,
And seeing, in the annexe beyond, M. play
A prelude of Bach on his harpsichord.

I can see his face now, heavy and numb
with resignation to the powers that come
At his touch meticulous, smooth as satin,
Firm as hammers: I can hear the air thrum
With notes like sun-motes in a twinkling pattern.

Her task there fetched from the girl the innate
Tingling response of glass to a note:
She fitted the moment, too, like a glove,
Who deft and submissive knelt by the grate
Bowed as if in the labour of love.

Their orbits touched not: but the pure submission
Of each gave value and definition
To a snapshot printed in that morning's sun.
From any odd corner we may start a vision
Proving that one and one make One.

C DAY LEWIS *One and one make One*

It is in the Book of Common Prayer that the word unity takes on a deeper meaning when it refers to the joining together of a man and a woman in holy matrimony 'signifying the mystical union that is betwixt Christ and his Church'.

The German poet Rilke spoke of 'love which consists in this, that two solitudes meet and greet and protect one another' – which is a more romantic way of saying that the union of marriage consists in the mutual society, help and comfort that the one ought to have of the other both in prosperity and adversity, and if a marriage has been built on such a foundation it won't matter if the rains descend and the floods come and the winds blow and beat upon the house; for it was founded on a rock.

Let me not to the marriage of true minds
Admit impediments. Love is not love
Which alters when it alteration finds,
Or bends with the remover to remove:
O, no! it is an ever-fixed mark
That looks on tempests and is never shaken;
It is the star to every wandering bark,
Whose worth's unknown, although his height be taken.
Love's not time's fool, though rosy lips and cheeks
Within his bending sickle's compass come;
Love alters not with his brief hours and weeks,
But bears it out even to the edge of doom.
If this be error, and upon me proved,
I never writ, nor no man ever loved.

SHAKESPEARE *Sonnet 116*

'Signifying the mystical union that is betwixt Christ and his Church' . . . between God and man. The mystic, the contemplative, who is shut off from the world by the walls of a monastery or convent, is rightly able to spend much time in trying to achieve this mystical union with God. But let us never imagine that union with God is easily achieved, even by the most saintly recluse.

Cardinal Hume, when he was Abbot of Ampleforth, often spoke to his monastic community on this theme; and we too can find comfort in his words.

> Let me remind you that when you feel God's absence, Christ our Lord, our model and our hope, experienced just this. There is a rhythm of light and darkness. Happily the memory of light enables us to support the darkness, to look forward to

the re-emergence of light. For there *is* light, and plenty of it. It comes by the initiative of God himself. Our task is to be faithful, to persevere, to respond. In proportion as we give, in proportion as we commit ourselves, in proportion as we pray and are humble, in proportion as we draw closer to God, he will bless us and guide us.

CARDINAL BASIL HUME *Searching for God*

It is hardly possible to imagine anyone less like Cardinal Hume than D H Lawrence, who in his stormy, restless life revolted against conventional Christianity; yet in his last poems, when he had come to terms with the imminence of his own early death, he was saying much the same thing about this rhythm of light and darkness in our attempts to draw closer to God.

And if tonight my soul may find her peace
in sleep, and sink in good oblivion,
and in the morning wake like a new-opened flower
then I have been dipped again in God, and new-created.
And if, as weeks go round, in the dark of the moon
my spirit darkens and goes out, and soft strange gloom
pervades my movements and my thoughts and words
then I shall know that I am walking still with God,
we are close together now the moon's in shadow.

. . .

And if, in the changing phases of man's life
I fall in sickness and in misery
my wrists seem broken and my heart seems dead
and strength is gone, and my life
is only the leavings of a life:

. . .

then I must know that still
I am in the hands of the unknown God,
he is breaking me down to his own oblivion
to send me forth on a new morning, a new man.

D H LAWRENCE from *Shadows*

> I was an hungered, and ye gave me meat: I was thirsty, and ye gave me drink: I was a stranger, and ye took me in:
> Naked, and ye clothed me: I was in prison, and ye came unto me.
>
> MATTHEW 25.35-36

'V' for visitors, visiting, visitations. My dictionary gives the verb to visit three broad meanings. The commonest is to go and see a person or a place as a social and, by implication, pleasurable exercise. It also means to carry out an inspection, to make an official visit. And finally there is the singularly unpleasant, but fortunately archaic, meaning of inflicting punishment. 'He visits the sins of the fathers upon the children.'

One of the most touching incidents in the Bible is the visitation made by the Virgin Mary after she has received the news not only of the approaching birth of Jesus, but also that her old cousin Elizabeth is having a child too, and she goes rushing off to share it all with her.

> And it came to pass, that, when Elizabeth heard the salutation of Mary, the babe leapt in her womb; and Elizabeth was filled with the Holy Ghost: and she spake out with a loud voice, and said, Blessed art thou among women and blessed is the fruit of thy womb.
>
> LUKE 1.41-42

After Elizabeth had duly given birth to a son, poor Zacharias, the father, who had been struck dumb throughout her pregnancy, is suddenly released from his verbal bondage to pour out the exultant words of the Benedictus. In it he uses the verb to visit in yet another and splendidly positive sense: 'Blessed be the Lord God of Israel who has visited and redeemed his people.' As the poem unfolds, Zacharias foresees the role of his own child John, as heralding the Messiah:

> And thou, child, shalt be called the prophet of the Highest; for thou shalt go before the face of the Lord to prepare his ways; to give knowledge of salvation unto his people for the remission of their sins, through the tender mercy of our God; whereby the dayspring from on high hath visited us, to give light to them that sit in darkness and in the shadow of death, and to guide our feet into the way of peace.
>
> LUKE 1.76-79

It is a pity that the word 'visitor' has become debased over the years. Because of the increase in bureaucracy it suggests nosey-parkerdom, form-filling, in-depth interviews, somebody from the town-hall. It is an image as unattractive as that summoned up by the now outmoded custom of leaving visiting-cards, which were left not from any love towards a new neighbour but as part of the protocol of a rigid class system. The very words 'visiting hours' outside a hospital instantly suggest bunches of rather sterile flowers and bright conversation round the bedside.

And yet when Christ says: 'I was sick and ye visited me. I was in prison and ye came to me' the word is restored and takes on again its compassionate meaning.

Among his more recent work, Charles Causley has written a sequence of poems called 'Ten Hospital Visitors' – penetrating studies from life observed during the many hours he must have spent in a public ward visiting his dying mother. Two of them stand out as contrasting patterns of behaviour. Firstly the self-righteous do-gooder whom St James surely had in mind when he wrote:

> If any man among you seem to be religious and bridleth not

his tongue, but deceiveth his own heart, this man's religion is vain.

JAMES 1.26

The first enters wearing the neon armour
Of virtue.
Ceaselessly firing all-purpose smiles
At everybody present
She destroys hope
In the breasts of the sick
Who realise instantly
That they are incapable of surmounting
Her ferocious goodwill

Such courage she displays
In the face of human disaster!

Fortunately she does not stay long.
After a speedy trip round the ward
In the manner of a nineteen-thirties destroyer
Showing the flag in the Mediterranean,
She returns home for a week
– With luck, longer –
Scorched by the heat of her own worthiness.

CHARLES CAUSLEY from *Ten Hospital Visitors*

And the other one in blessed contrast, the person of quiet compassion for whom St James has an equally apt description.

Pure religion and undefiled before God and the Father is this, To visit the fatherless and widows in their affliction, and to keep himself unspotted from the world.

JAMES 1.27

The sixth visitor says little,
Breathes reassurance,

Smiles securely.
Carries no black passport of grapes
And visa of chocolate. Has a clutch
Of clean washing.

Unobtrusively stows it
In the locker; searches out more.
Talks quietly to the Sister
Out of sight, out of earshot, of the patient.
Arrives punctually as a tide.
Does not stay the whole hour.

Even when she has gone
The patient seems to sense her there:
An upholding
Presence.

CHARLES CAUSLEY from *Ten Hospital Visitors*

It is rather sad that with fewer people going to church nowadays they do not seek the spiritual care of their local priest or pastor. Let us hope that this role of the clergy as pastoral visitors will never be taken over by computers or spiritual clinics, however discouraged and inadequate many of them must feel at the enormity of their problem and the little they can do; a feeling so starkly expressed by the Reverend R S Thomas in one of his poems:

Evans? Yes, many a time
I came down his bare flight
Of stairs into the gaunt kitchen
With its wood fire, where crickets sang
Accompaniment to the black kettle's
Whine, and so into the cold
Dark to smother in the thick tide
Of night that drifted about the walls
Of his stark farm on the hill ridge.

It was not the dark filling my eyes
And mouth appalled me; not even the drip
Of rain like blood from the one tree
Weather-tortured. It was the dark
Silting the veins of that sick man
I left stranded upon the vast
And lonely shore of his bleak bed.

R S THOMAS *Evans*

It's difficult not to look back nostalgically to those peaceful days a hundred years ago when there seemed to be more time for pastoral visiting – visits so vividly described by the Reverend Francis Kilvert who would walk miles over the roughest country in any weather. Visits like his one to the old man James Jones who had once dabbled in witchcraft and to whom he was able to bring his 'upholding presence'.

29th April 1876

A day of unceasing, hopeless rain. I spent the morning in the village. Amongst other people I went to see the old wizard James Jones and his wife . . . The wizard lay upstairs in bed very weak and ill, perhaps dying. He seemed very happy and peaceful and quite content. The days of magic and necromancy had gone by and he had emerged from the atmosphere of charms, incantations, astrology and witchcraft a simple, humble, childlike Christian man. The old wizard took my hand lovingly and most tenderly, touchingly, and affectionately he gave me his blessing and wished me Godspeed. 'You have done great good in this place,' he said. 'You have been a blessing to this place'. Then with his withered shrunken hand and arm and raising his eyes solemnly to heaven the dying necromancer called to God to witness that he died in charity with all men. 'I wish no one any harm,' he said. 'I am at peace with all the world.' And so we parted, never perhaps to meet again in this world.

FRANCIS KILVERT

O God, thou art my God; early will I seek thee. My soul thirsteth for thee; my flesh longeth for thee in a dry and thirsty land where no water is.

PSALM 63.1

In the wilderness shall waters break out, and streams in the desert. And the parched ground shall become a pool, and the thirsty land springs of water.

ISAIAH 35.6-7

The Bible is full of references to water. In ancient Palestine shortage of water resulted in drought and famine as a recurrent menace, rainfall was seen as a sign of God's favour and goodness; and when the Psalmist makes a list of God's blessings the most seductive one is that 'He shall feed me in a green pasture, and lead me forth by the waters of comfort'.

Water is symbolic of refreshment not only in the physical sense of quenching the thirst but also in the deeper sense of satisfying a spiritual longing. These two meanings are never more profoundly illustrated than in Christ's compassionate encounter with the woman of Samaria, at the well of Sychar when He asks her for water to drink.

Then saith the woman of Samaria unto him, How is it that thou, being a Jew, askest drink of me, which am a woman of Samaria? for the Jews have no dealings with the Samaritans.

Jesus answered and said unto her, If thou knewest the gift of God, and who it is that saith to thee, Give me to drink; thou wouldest have asked him, and he would have given thee living water.
The woman saith unto him, Sir, thou hast nothing to draw with, and the well is deep: from whence then hast thou that living water?
Art thou greater than our father Jacob, which gave us the well, and drank thereof himself, and his children, and his cattle?
Jesus answered and said unto her, Whosoever drinketh of this water shall thirst again:
But whosoever drinketh of the water that I shall give him shall never thirst; but the water that I shall give him shall be in him a well of water springing up into everlasting life.

JOHN 4.9-14

Water is also symbolic of cleansing, and once again there are the two aspects – spiritual and physical; the physical cleansing of the body when it is tired and dirtied by toil and travel.

In one of the most remarkable of all his poems Gerard Manley Hopkins describes how on a summer's walk he reached a moorland stream cascading down from the heights between overhanging branches where he hears the shouts of a party of boys bathing in a rock pool in timeless happiness.

Hark, hearer, hear what I do; lend a thought now,
make believe
We are leafwhelmed somewhere with the hood
Of some branchy, bunchy bushybowered wood,
Southern dene or Lancashire clough or Devon
cleave,
That leans along the loins of hills, where a
candycoloured, where a bluegold-brown
Marbled river, boisterously beautiful, between
Roots and rocks is danced and dandled, all in froth
and water-blowballs, down.

We are there, when we hear a shout
That the hanging honeysuck, the dogeared hazels in
  the cover
Makes dither, makes hover
And the riot of a rout
Of, it must be, boys from the town
Bathing: it is summer's sovereign good.

By there comes a listless stranger; beckoned by the
  noise
He drops towards the river: unseen
Sees the bevy of them, how the boys
With dare and with downdolphinry and bellbright
  bodies huddling out,
Are earthworld, airworld, waterworld thorough
  hurled, all by turn and turn about . . .

The temptation to follow their example is irresistible and he walks on until he finds an equally secluded pool among the rocks where he takes off his clothes.

Till walk the world he can with bare his feet
And come where lies a coffer, burly of all blocks
Built of chancequarried, selfquained rocks
And the water warbles over into, filleted with
  glassy grassy quicksilvery shives and shoots
And with heavenfallen freshness down from
  moorland still brims,
Dark or daylight on and on. Here he will then,
  here he will the fleet
Flinty kindcold element let break across his limbs
Long. Where we leave him, froliclavish while he
  looks about him, laughs, swims.

GERARD MANLEY HOPKINS from *Epithalamion*

There is also the cleansing of the spirit by the living water which enables us to 'turn from our wickedness and live', like the prostitute who 'stood at Jesus' feet behind Him weeping, and began to wash His feet with tears.' Nearer our own time there were the young soldiers of the First World War who before their idealism was so cruelly betrayed saw it as an opportunity to cleanse the spirit.

Now, God be thanked who has matched us with
His hour,
And caught our youth, and wakened us from
sleeping,
With hand made sure, clear eye, and sharpened
power,
To turn, as swimmers into cleanness leaping,
Glad from a world grown old and cold and weary,
Leave the sick hearts that honour could not
move,
And half-men, with their dirty songs and dreary,
And all the little emptiness of love!

Oh! we, who have known shame, we have found
release there,
Where there's no ill, no grief, but sleep has
mending,
Naught broken save this body, lost but
breath;
Nothing to shake the laughing heart's long peace
there
But only agony, and that has ending;
And the worst friend and enemy is but Death.

RUPERT BROOKE *Peace*

In the creation story God decrees that the waters under the heaven be gathered together into one place and that the dry land appear. And God called the dry land earth, and the gathering together of the waters called he seas. And a little later he sent up a mist from the earth and watered the whole face of the ground. And with that matchless imagery the pattern of seedtime and harvest has been set immemorially with our dependence on water as the primary source of all our nourishment. So each year as the annual cycle of growth is completed with the last of the autumn crops we can praise God for the gift of water and echo the words of the Psalmist.

> Thou visitest the earth, and waterest it: thou greatly enrichest it with the river of God, which is full of water: thou preparest them corn, when thou hast so provided for it.
> Thou waterest the ridges thereof abundantly: thou settlest the furrows thereof: thou makest it soft with showers: thou blessest the springing thereof.
> Thou crownest the year with thy goodness; and thy paths drop fatness.
> They drop upon the pastures of the wilderness: and the little hills rejoice on every side.
> The pastures are clothed with flocks; the valleys also are covered over with corn; they shout for joy, they also sing.
>
> PSALM 65.9-13

O Lord, thou hast searched me, and known me.
Thou knowest my downsitting and mine uprising, thou understandest my thought afar off.
Thou compassest my path and my lying down, and art acquainted with all my ways.
For there is not a word in my tongue, but, lo, O Lord, Thou knowest it altogether.
Thou hast beset me behind and before, and laid thine hand upon me.
Such knowledge is too wonderful for me; it is high, I cannot attain unto it.

PSALM 139.1-6

What do you do when you come to the letter 'X'? It would be uncharitable to devote a whole chapter to xenophobia, 'the irrational fear of foreigners or strangers', though it is rather nice when the tourists go home and leave us to content ourselves alone through the winter. At home when we play The Parson's Cat everybody falls about with laughter on reaching the letter 'X' – trying to get away with: The Parson's Cat is an excellent cat or an ecstatic cat and of course one has to cheat a bit. So 'X' is the algebraic unknown quantity, 'X' is the symbol for the unsolved mystery, the endless question-marks of Why and How and When which we associate in the first place with what is now fashionably called the paranormal.

First to describe the house. Who has not seen it
once at the end of an evening's walk – the
leaves

that suddenly open, and as sudden screen it
with the first flickering hint of shadowy eaves?

Was there a light in the high window? Or
only the moon's cool candle palely lit?
Was there a pathway leading to the door?
Or only grass and none to walk on it?

And surely someone cried, 'Who goes there –
Who?'
And ere the lips could shape the whispered 'I'
the same voice rose and chuckled 'You, tis You!'
A voice, or the furred night-owl's human cry?

Who has not seen the house? Who has not started
towards the gate half-seen, and paused,
half-fearing,
and half beyond all fear – and the leaves parted
again, and there was nothing in the clearing?

HUMBERT WOLFE *The House of Ghosts*

Ghosts, haunted houses, telepathy, and so on, are mysteries over which we can speculate endlessly, and the extent to which we can find our own emotional response to them or they can be revealed to us by rational argument is of little consequence. Just as the zoologists and botanists and biochemists can explain to us the complex phenomena of plant and animal life, yet they still remain in the final analysis, mysteries.

How do you know, deep underground,
Hid in your bed from sight and sound,
Without a turn in temperature,
With weather life can scarce endure,
That light has won a fraction's strength
And day put on some moment's length,

Whereof in merest rote will come,
Weeks hence, mild airs that do not numb?
  O crocus root, how do you know,
    How do you know?

THOMAS HARDY from *The Year's Awakening*

These are all lesser mysteries which may absorb us or leave us quite indifferent. Some people can devote a life-time of research into the sex-life of some obscure order of insects, others into whether Bacon wrote Shakespeare; while to the incurious man 'a primrose by a river's brim, a yellow primrose is to him, and nothing more.'

It is the greater mysteries of life and death which afford no clear-cut answer, that tease and baffle us. The mystery of death is one which we accept with a degree of equanimity in proportion to the strength of our faith, because we know that 'there is no road but hath an end.' We accept death for ourselves, but it is terribly difficult to accept when a young child is killed or struck down by some wasting disease, or, as in this poem, a much wanted baby is still-born.

What ceremony can we fit
You into now? If you had come
Out of a warm and noisy room
To this, there'd be an opposite
For us to know you by. We could
Imagine you in lively mood

And then look at the other side,
The mood drawn out of you, the breath
Defeated by the power of death,
But we have never seen you stride
Ambitiously the world we know.
You could not come and yet you go.

But there is nothing now to mar
Your clear refusal of our world.
Not in our memories can we mould
You or distort your character.
Then all our consolation is
That grief can be as pure as this.

ELIZABETH JENNINGS *To a Child born Dead*

It is the mysteries of life that defeat us – the mystery of a world of increasing violence, cruelty, greed and injustice watched over by a loving God who sees the little sparrow fall. The bishop who argues the case for belief in Browning's poem sums it up.

'There the old misgivings, crooked questions are –
This good God, What he could do if he would,
Would, if he could . . . '

ROBERT BROWNING from
Bishop Blougram's Apology

How can it be that God can reign in glory
Calmly content with what His love has done,
Reading unmoved the piteous shameful story,
All the vile deeds men do beneath the sun?

Are there no tears in the heart of the Eternal?
Is there no pain to pierce the soul of God?
Then must he be fiend of Hell infernal,
Beating the earth to pieces with His rod.

Father, if He, the Christ *were* the revealer,
Truly the first begotten of the Lord,
Then must Thou be a sufferer and a healer,
Pierced to the heart by the sorrow of the sword.

Then must it mean, not only that the sorrow

Smote Thee that once upon the lonely tree,
But that today, tonight and on the morrow
Still it will come, O gallant God to Thee.

G A STUDDART KENNEDY *How can it be?*

That poem by Studdart Kennedy, written in the agony of the trenches on the Western Front, goes some way to answering the unanswerable; but the harsh yet comforting truth has been put even more starkly by George Mcleod.

Why undeserved suffering? My God, why? The Church doesn't know the answer. Christ doesn't tell us the answer: what Christ does is to face the suffering. He knew all our sorrows. He suffered undeservedly. Faced with this ghastly problem of undeserved suffering in His own experience, He identified himself with the mystery: He brought Himself to say 'My God, why?'. But this cry of dereliction was not his last cry on the Cross. Just before He died He said a very different word. Still on the Cross, still suffering, He said a very different word. He said 'Father, into thy hands I commend my spirit'.

G F MACLEOD

Remember now thy creator, in the days of thy youth, while the evil days come not, nor the years draw nigh when thou shalt say, I have no pleasure in them.

ECCLESIASTES 12.1

Rejoice O young man in thy youth, and and let thy heart cheer thee in the days of thy youth, and walk in the ways of thine heart and in the sight of thine eyes.

ECCLESIASTES 11.9

When I was a child, I spake as a child, I understood as a child, I thought as a child; but when I became a man I put away childish things. For now we see through a glass, darkly; but then face to face: for now I know in part; but then shall I know even as also I am known.

I CORINTHIANS 13.11-12

'Y' is for youth and I suppose it could be for yearning as well, because as you grow older and have long ago put away childish things youth seems so transient, so vulnerable. Yet to the young themselves it seems unending and they answer our questions with touching confidence:

Tell me tell me, smiling child,
What the Past is like to thee.
– An Autumn evening soft and mild
With a wind that sighs mournfully.

Tell me what is the Present hour.
– A green and flowery spray,
Where a young bird sits gathering its power
To mount and fly away.

And what is the Future, happy one?
– A sea beneath a cloudless sun:
A mighty glorious dazzling sea
Stretching into Infinity.

EMILY BRONTE *Tell Me, Tell Me, Smiling Child*

But of course it's nothing of the sort; youth doesn't stretch into infinity, and the sea doesn't remain calm for long:

All lovely things will have an ending,
All lovely things will fade and die,
And youth, that's now so bravely spending,
Will beg a penny bye and bye.

Fine ladies all are soon forgotten,
And golden-rod is dust when dead,
The sweetest flesh and flowers are rotten
And cobwebs tent the brightest head.

Come back, true love! Sweet Youth return!
But time goes on and will, unheeding,
Though hands will reach, and eyes will yearn,
And the wild days set true hearts bleeding.

Come back, true love! Sweet Youth remain!
But golden-rod and daisies wither,
And over them blows autumn rain,
They pass, they pass, and know not whither.

CONRAD AIKEN *All Lovely Things*

We know that time *will* in the end set true hearts bleeding and there is precious little we can do except to surround them with our love. 'You cannot save them from the test they're made for, but hug them to your heart, and heaven prayed for.'

And a woman who held a babe against her bosom said,
Speak to us of children.
And he said,
Your children are not *your* children.
They are the sons and daughters of Life's longing
for itself.
They come through you but not from you,
And though they are with you yet they belong not
to you.

You may give them your love but not your
thoughts,
For they have their own thoughts.
You may house their bodies but not their souls,
For their souls dwell in the house of tomorrow,
which you cannot visit, not even in your dreams,
You may strive to be like them, but seek not to
make them like you.
For life goes not backward nor tarries with
yesterday.

KAHLIL GIBRAN *On Children*

'You may give them your love but not your thoughts, for they have their own thoughts.'

We live in our own world,
A world that is too small
For you to stoop and enter
Even on hands and knees,
The adult subterfuge.
And though you probe and pry

With analytic eye
And eavesdrop all our talk
With an amused look,
You cannot find the centre
Where we dance, where we play,
Where Life is still asleep
Under the closed flower,
Under the smooth shell
Of eggs in the cupped nest
That mock the faded blue
Of your remoter heaven.

R S THOMAS *Children's Song*

We cannot find the centre where they dance, where they play but it is comforting to remember that their world is not too small for Christ to stoop and enter.

> They brought children for him to lay his hands on them with prayer. The disciples scolded them for it, but Jesus said to them, Let the children come to me; do not stop them, for the kingdom of Heaven belongs to these.

MATTHEW 19.13-14

'Life goes not backwards nor tarries with yesterday,' and so it is unworthy to envy the young, and useless to look back with longing for the past. Siegfried Sassoon struck the right balance in one of his poems.

When I was young my heart and head were light,
And I was gay and feckless as a colt
Out in the fields, with morning in the may,
Wind on the grass, wings in the orchard bloom.
O thrilling sweet, my joy, when life was free,
And all the paths led on from hawthorn-time
Across the carolling meadows into June.

But now my heart is heavy-laden. I sit
Burning my dreams away beside the fire:

For death has made me wise and bitter and strong;
And I am rich in all that I have lost.
    O starshine on the fields of long ago,
    Bring me the darkness and the nightingale;
    Dim wealds of vanished summer, peace of
      home,
And silence; and the faces of my friends.

SIEGFRIED SASSOON *Memory*

As we get older it is sometimes possible to see in the glass less darkly; to see a pattern unfolding in which our childhood and youth, and the lives of our own children and of their children who will live long after we are dead are all woven into the design. John Drinkwater, in his poem, put it very simply.

Lovers, a little of this your happy time
Give to the thought of us who were as you,
That we, whose dearest passion in your prime
Is but a winter garment, may renew
Our love in yours, our flesh in your desire,
Our tenderness in your discovering kiss,
For we are half the fuel of your fire,
As ours was fed by Marc and Beatrice.
Remember us, and, when you too are dead,
Our prayer with yours shall fall upon love's spring
That all our ghostly loves be comforted
In those yet later lovers' love-making;
So shall oblivion bring his dust to spill
On brain and limbs, and we be lovers still.

JOHN DRINKWATER *To the Lovers That Come After Us*

Z

I am Alpha and Omega, The Beginning and the End, saith the Lord, which is and which was and which is to come, the Almighty.

REVELATION 1.8

And ye shall hear of wars and rumours of wars: see that ye be not troubled: for all these things must come to pass, but the end is not yet.

MATTHEW 24.6

It seems incredible that it is over sixty years since the signing of the armistice which marked the ending of the most terrible of all wars; most terrible despite man's subsequent efforts to exterminate his fellows by more sophisticated methods than trench warfare.

I remember that grey wet November day in 1918 with great clarity. As a small boy I had been taken shopping, not that there was much to buy, and suddenly I became aware that everybody seemed to have gone mad. People started singing and dancing in the streets, brother clasped the hand of brother, the war was over:

Everyone suddenly burst out singing;
And I was filled with such delight
As prisoned birds must find in freedom,
Winging wildly across the white

Orchards and dark-green fields; on – on – and
out of sight.
Everyone's voice was suddenly lifted;
And beauty came like the setting sun;
My heart was shaken with tears; and horror
Drifted away . . . O, but Everyone
Was a bird; and the song was wordless; the singing
will never be done.

SIEGFRIED SASSOON *Everyone Sang*

Horror didn't drift away for very long. Wilfred Owen, perhaps the greatest of the war poets, who was killed only a few days before the signing of that armistice, had prophesied in one of his poems that 'better men would come and greater wars'. And twenty-one years later we were at war again, fighting the same enemy for the same cause.

And even the atom bomb which still threatens to finish all life as we understand it has not prevented the bitter wars of emerging nationalism, of sectarian hatreds, which still rage or smoulder dangerously today. But however dark the future seems in our moments of despondency life still goes on. We go on believing with Gerard Manley Hopkins that . . . 'Nature is never spent. There lives the dearest freshness deep down things.' We still fall in love and marry and bring children into the world.

Only a man harrowing clods
In a slow silent walk
With an old horse that stumbles and nods
Half asleep as they stalk.

Only thin smoke without flame
From the heaps of couch-grass;
Yet this will go onward the same
Though Dynasties pass.

Yonder a maid and her wight
  Come whispering by;
War's annals will cloud into night
  Ere their story die.

THOMAS HARDY *At the Time of the Breaking of Nations*

That poem by Thomas Hardy says it all with an extraordinary economy of words. He wrote it in 1915, but the idea for the poem came to him forty-five years earlier when he was walking in the remote, peaceful countryside of North Cornwall with the girl with whom he had just fallen in love. It was during the hot dry summer of 1870, as the news was coming through of the shattering defeat of France in the Franco-Prussian war – that first dark shadow of the shape of things to come.

This heroic detachment of men and women from the great tides of history, from the wars and dynastic upheavals which are beyond their control is a recurring theme in all literature. A hundred years before the birth of Christ a Chinese general wrote this valedictory poem to his wife:

I am going on service away to the battleground
And I do not know when I shall come back.
I hold your hand with only a deep sigh;
Afterwards — tears — in the days when we are
  parted.
With all your might enjoy the spring flowers
But do not forget the time of our love and pride.
Know that if I live I will come back again
And if I die, we will go on thinking of each other.

GENERAL SU WU *The General*

Where that battleground was, and who won or lost, is one of war's annals that has clouded into night. But that love poem is indestructible. It is a poem which would have pleased Edward Thomas, that other poet of the First World War, who expressed the same heroic detachment in the last letter which he wrote to his beloved wife Helen just before he was killed by the blast from a shell at the battle of Arras:

> Arras. Easter 1917
> My dear, you must not ask me to say too much. I know that you must say much because you feel much. But I, you see, must not feel anything. I am just as it were tunnelling under ground and something sensible in my subconscious directs me not to think of the sun; at the end of the tunnel there is the sun.
> Here I am in my valise on the floor of my dug-out writing before sleeping. The artillery is like a stormy tide on the shores of the full-moon that rides high and clear among white cirrus clouds. I thought today would be a bad day, but we did all the shelling. Hardly anything came near the observation post. I simply watched the shells changing the landscape. The village among the trees that I saw two weeks ago is now just ruins among violated stark tree trunks. But the sun shone and larks and partidges made love and the trench was being made passable for the wounded that will be harvested in a day or two . . . We shall be enormously busy now. It will be all work till further notice. So goodnight and I hope you sleep no worse than I do.

Perhaps these memories of the First World War are rather too sombre a note on which to end and the Psalmist strikes a more hopeful note.

> 'He maketh wars to cease unto the end of the earth;
> He breaketh the bow, and cutteth the spear in sunder;
> He burneth the chariot in the fire'.

So let us not weave patterns of sound round words like zealous and zestful or any other terminal attributes of The Parson's Cat; instead, here is a poem by D H Lawrence, remembering that in the last resort the parson's cat is a peaceful cat:

All that matters is to be at one with the living God
to be a creature in the house of the God of life.

Like a cat asleep on a chair
at peace, in peace
And at one with the master of the house, with the
mistress,

at home, at home in the house of the living,
sleeping on the hearth and yawning before the fire.

Sleeping on the hearth of the living world
yawning at home before the fire of life
feeling the presence of the living God
like a great reassurance
a deep calm in the heart
a presence
as of the master sitting at the board
in his own and greater being,
in the house of life.

D H LAWRENCE *Pax*

Postscript

'SURE AS TOMORROW MORNING'

One of my dreariest recollections of the rather dreary school at which I was supposed to be educated was an exercise known as 'rep'.

The master who took it was an ardent gardener with a flair for combining business with pleasure and he would summon us to his garden, one at a time, in all weathers to reel off the prescribed five hundred lines, cut straight from the joint as it were, of Milton or Keats or whoever, which we had laboriously committed to memory.

Bent double over his beloved rockery or immersed in his border he would occasionally grunt or wince as the performance droned on, though whether from the ineptitude of our delivery or the intransigence of his soil was never really clear.

Fortunately this sterile activity did not kill my love for poetry which I was able to discover for myself in later years, but it did leave me with a permanent inability to memorise it. Except, that is, for individual lines or couplets which have fixed themselves unaided in my mind like mounted butterflies, because of their haunting beauty or their quality of magic, or their capacity to distil, as William Blake could, a whole philosophy into a tight little string of words like:

> To see a world in a grain of sand.

And I never know when one of them, which may have lain

dormant for years, will suddenly come fluttering up from the unconscious, released perhaps by some sight or sound or smell.

Just before dusk in late September when you have banked up your bonfire of dead leaves before coming in for the night and you suddenly know that the long summer is ending, out flies Shakespeare's marvellous line

> The bright day is done, and we are for the dark.

But some of them are never far below the surface and for me as I get older that line of de la Mare's constantly occurs.

> Look thy last on all things lovely
> Every hour

Words which combine beauty and magic and the distilled essence of all that really needs to be said about the passing of youth, the fading of beauty, the wild acceleration of the hands of the clock, the inevitability of death.

I find them immensely comforting and they purge me of the poison of self-pity. Perhaps this *is* my last bonfire, my last sunset. Thank God I don't know, but let me savour it, extract every ounce of pleasure from it as though it was. And then everything seems to fall into place; the past, the present, even the future: because whatever the after-life holds for me my children will live after me as I have lived after my parents.

Of all the butterflies in my collection some of the most precious have been hatched from Gerard Manley Hopkins who has been my constant companion since I first discovered his poetry early on in the Second World War.

No one has expressed more movingly the loneliness of an austere and celibate faith combined with a wild intoxication with the boundless beauty of nature

> Glory be to God for dappled things –
> For skies of couple-colour as a brinded cow;

No one has been more deeply concerned with the age-old problem, more relevant and urgent than ever in this conservation era of how

> to keep
> Back beauty, keep it, beauty, beauty, beauty
> from vanishing away.

So when winter approaches and we are for the dark, I shall go on looking my last on all things lovely, and if some moment comes, as it will, when there really doesn't seem to be anything lovely to look on at all but only fog and freezing and frustration and no end of it in sight, there may be a sudden burst of winter sunshine and one of Gerard Manley Hopkins' bright-winged butterflies will fly up again into the warmth

> Sure as that spring primroses
> Shall new dapple next year – sure as tomorrow
> morning

and my fog and frustration will vanish with it into the upper air.

Acknowledgements

The publishers would like to acknowledge their use of copyright material from the following publications:
'Napoleon' and 'Keep Innocency' by Walter de la Mare, reprinted by permission of the Literary Trustees of Walter de la Mare and The Society of Authors as their representative: 'Pyrenean' by J B Morton, Longman Group Limited, reprinted by permission of A D Peters & Co. Ltd: *The Light of Christ* by Evelyn Underhill, Longman Group Limited: 'Memory', 'Devotion to Duty', 'Everyone Sang', 'Morning' by Siegfried Sassoon, reprinted by permission of George Sassoon: 'March Morning Unlike Others' by Ted Hughes, reprinted by permission of Faber and Faber Ltd from *Season Songs* by Ted Hughes: 'Tall Nettles' by Edward Thomas, reprinted from *Collected Poems* by Edward Thomas, by permission of Faber and Faber Ltd.: *World Without End* by Helen Thomas, reprinted by permission of Faber and Faber Ltd and Myfanwy Thomas: 'I Think Continually of Those Who Were Truly Great' by Stephen Spender, reprinted by permission of Faber and Faber Ltd, from *Collected Poems* by Stephen Spender: 'The Parable of the Old Men and the Young' by Wilfred Owen, from the *Collected Poems* of Wilfred Owen edited by Sean Day Lewis, reprinted by permission of the literary estate of Wilfred Owen and Chatto & Windus Ltd: 'Shadows', 'Piano' and 'Pax' by D H Lawrence, from *The Complete Poems* by D H Lawrence, William Heinemann Ltd, reprinted by permission of Lawrence Pollinger Ltd and the Estate of the late Mrs Frieda Lawrence Ravagli: 'Children's Song', 'Evans' and 'The Country Clergy' by R S Thomas from *Song of the Years' Turning* and *Poetry for Supper*, Granada Publishing Ltd: 'Mary of Bethany' from *The Witnesses* by Clive Sansom, Methuen: *Helena* by Evelyn Waugh, Chapman and Hall, reprinted by permission of A D Peters and Co. Ltd: *Journey for a Soul* by George Appleton, Collins: 'Not Love Perhaps' and 'Daydream' by A J S Tessimond, from *Not Love Perhaps*, Autolycus Press, reprinted by permission of Hubert Nicholson: 'In the Children's Room' by Tony Connor from *Kon in Spring Time*, Oxford University Press, 1968, is used with the author's permission: *The Towers of Trebizond* by Rose Macauley, reprinted by permission of A D Peters & Co. Ltd: 'To the Lovers That Come After Us' and 'Olton Pools' by John Drinkwater, Sidgwick & Jackson: 'The Cry of Earth's Anguish Went Up to God' by C L Drawbridge, taken from *The Mystery of Suffering* by Hugh Evan Hopkins, Inter-Varsity Press: 'The Storm-Cone' and 'Gethsemene' by Rudyard Kipling, reprinted by permission of The National Trust of Great Britain, Eyre Metheun Limited, and A P Watt Ltd.: 'David' by Alfred Duff Cooper, Granada Publishing Limited: G F Macleod, quoted in *From Darkness to Light* by Victor Gollancz, Victor Gollancz Ltd: 'Lot 96', 'A Marriage Song', 'O Dreams, O Destinations', 'One and one Make One', 'Annunciation: Leonardo' by C Day Lewis from *Collected Poems*, Jonathan Cape Ltd and the Hogarth Press, reprinted by permission of the Executors of the Estate of C Day Lewis: Twenty lines from 'Prayer

for His Fellow Prisoners, Christmas 1943', beginning with the line 'Lord Jesus Christ' by Dietrich Bonhoeffer from *Letters and Papers from Prison*, the Enlarged Edition, SCM Press 1971, p 140: 'How Can It Be?' by G A Studdart Kennedy, reprinted by permission of Hodder & Stoughton Ltd.: *Searching for God* by Basil Hume, reprinted by permission of Hodder & Stoughton Ltd.: 'Singing in the Streets' by Leonard Clark, from *Poems for Christmas*, Dennis Dobson: 'The House of Ghosts' from *This Blind Rose* by Humbert Wolfe is quoted by permission of Miss Ann Wolfe: 'Ten Hospital Visitors' by Charles Causley from *Collected Poems*, Macmillan: 'A Considerable Speck' by Robert Frost from *The Poetry of Robert Frost* edited by Edward Connery Latham, Jonathan Cape Ltd, reprinted by permission of the Estate of Robert Frost: 'On Children' from *The Prophet* by Kahlil Gibran, Alfred A Knopf, Inc.: 'The Enemies' and 'For a Child Born Dead' by Elizabeth Jennings, from *Collected Poems*, Macmillan, reprinted by permission of David Higham Associates Ltd: *The Shropshire Lad* by A E Housman, Harrap, reprinted by permission of the Society of Authors: 'All Lovely Things' by Conrad Aiken, from *Collected Poems*, Oxford University Press.